*Secret Exodus*

# Secret Exodus

## CLAIRE SAFRAN

PRENTICE HALL PRESS • *New York*

Published by Prentice Hall Press
A Division of Simon & Schuster, Inc.
Gulf+Western Building
One Gulf+Western Plaza
New York, NY   10023

PRENTICE HALL PRESS is a trademark of Simon & Schuster, Inc.

Library of Congress Cataloging-in-Publication Data
Safran, Claire.
Secret exodus.

1. Falasha Rescue, 1984–1985. 2. Ethiopia—Emigration and immigration. 3.
Israel—Emigration and immigration. 4. Ethiopia—Ethnic relations. I. Title.
II. Title: Operation Moses.
DS135.E75S24   1987      362.8′7′089924063      87-12659
ISBN 978-1-4516-8374-5

Designed by Irving Perkins Associates

Manufactured in the United States of America

10 9 8 7 6 5 4 3 2 1

First Edition

*To John Milton Williams,*
*who knew the road to Jerusalem,*
*and to Scott,*
*who found his own way*

# Contents

# Introduction

OPERATION MOSES WAS a lifesaving conspiracy that reached across many borders. A curious band of master plotters—Americans, Israelis, Ethiopians, Sudanese, Europeans—came together to make it happen. It was a rare rescue, one that worked.

When it happened, there were stories around the world, reams of words, an explosion of headlines. Some of what was written then was true, some of it half true, much of it mistaken. Until now, this modern exodus had kept many of its secrets. Almost three years after its unlikely allies began to formulate their plans, the story can now be told.

It begins in an ancient mystery. For more than two thousand years the black Jews of Ethiopia, remnants of one of the lost tribes of Israel, preserved their heritage and their stubborn belief in the Old Testament prophecy that one day they would return to Jerusalem. In the 1970s, when a military junta assumed power in Ethiopia and began to persecute religious minorities, these people were more determined than ever to go back to their ancestral home. But emigration was barred, and the unofficial way out was paved with peril. Then the secret exodus began, a series of bold rescues that took place before, during, and after the clandestine airlift known as Operation Moses. Sixteen thousand men, women, and children were led to freedom, sometimes on foot, now and then by boat, mostly on "the wings of eagles."

*Who are these people?* When I first asked that question, I was a little child, peering down from the women's balcony in a small synagogue in Brooklyn, New York. Two black men had slipped into a rear pew. They didn't "look like Jews," but they acted like them, wrapped in prayer shawls, swaying back and forth in their worship. A murmur, a buzz of wonder, ran through the synagogue. When the service was over, there was no special greeting or welcome for these strangers. As quickly and quietly as they had arrived, they left.

Who are they? My father was a learned man, and I pestered him with questions. Ethiopians, he thought. Once he had heard of such a lost tribe. Were they Jews? Forgotten in Africa, how did they survive? My father shrugged. "How? Who knows how? But they did." It finished like most of our religious discussions. "In the end, there are only so many answers," he told me. "Then there is the mystery."

With Operation Moses, some of the enigma began to be solved. I flew to meet some of those desperate travelers. Typical, and also special, was a gaunt woman named Malka Alemie. From my first glimpse of her, Malka has haunted me. She sits in that Ethiopian stillness, only her hands fluttering like excited birds, dipping in despair, soaring in hope, circling in wonder at what has happened to her. She makes clicking sounds in the back of her throat, African punctuation for an amazing story. She has come from near death to new life. She has moved across continents and across centuries, out of a primitive village and into the twentieth century.

More of the story came from Gideon, a bony young conspirator with a sweet, gap-toothed smile. He is named for the falasha* kings who once ruled over large areas of Ethiopia, and he survived by turning himself into a prince of liars. He lived undercover, slipping across borders like a night shadow. Sometimes he joined forces with private American groups who ran free-lance rescues. Sometimes he linked up with the Israeli secret service. He was one of a handful of falashas who worked behind enemy lines. They led their brothers and sisters out of Ethiopia, helped keep them alive in the purgatory of Sudan, and finally spirited them on to the promised land.

"Be careful how you write this story," another conspirator warns me. He is a key official in the U.S. Department of State, still undercover, still hiding his leading role in one of our century's most daring rescues.

A good deed had been committed, but no one wanted to plead guilty to it. Quickly, the master planners ducked for cover. Operation Moses took brains and courage, but there were no medals or career promotions for those who dared to carry it out. Some people lost their jobs and some went to jail; some could lose their lives if their names were known.

In Sudan, it is high treason, punishable by death, to have been involved in Operation Moses. In Ethiopia, it is dangerous even to be related to someone who took part. To protect fathers and daughters, husbands and sisters who are still in Ethiopia, most of the black Jews I talked with asked me to use their Hebrew names, adopted in Israel, instead of their Ethiopian names. The events are true; the scenes and conversations have been reconstructed from the testimony of those who were there. But some people must be camouflaged even further, for special reasons. Gideon is a composite of two brave rescuers who hope to act again. Josef of Armachiho is a pseudonym for one of the bandit guides who still roam the mountains of Ethiopia and may lead still more people to freedom.

*In recent years, *Falasha* has come to be an insult. When we use the word *falasha,* without capitals, it is to describe that time and place where the Beta Israel lived a life of insult, in exile, as strangers and outcasts.

In Israel, there was euphoria over Operation Moses. After years of bad news, here was something unquestionably good, something joyful to celebrate. There was a national pride the people hadn't felt since the rescue at Entebbe. Yet many of the details are still censored there, for some good reasons and a few questionable ones. Some secrecy is still necessary, to make future rescues around the world possible. Some of the secrecy is political, to hide mistakes and save face.

For Americans, these are events to be proud of. The U.S. government dared to care about the human rights of these lost people, and Americans had the know-how and the daring to make the rescue fly. The United States had nothing to gain from Operation Moses and much to lose. Political influence and friendships in Africa and the Middle East were at risk. Because they are still important, American officials were tight-lipped and guarded about this rescue.

Yet the telling of this story is important, and I am grateful to those men and women who understood that silence can be a fool's gold. In Washington, clearance came from wise men at the top, so that key officials could talk to me about these events. In other American cities, then in Europe, Africa, and the Middle East, other people shared other pieces of the puzzle.

Each clue led to more people and more bits and pieces of the story. All sorts of people made the rescue happen, and they acted out of a mixed bag of motives—politics, money, ambition, adventure, the humanitarian instinct. Over the months, I met heroes and villains, brave ones and liars, saviors and the saved, Christians, Moslems, and Jews.

Unforgettably, I met Malka Alemie and her people, the mysterious Beta Israel. More than anything else, the secret exodus is a triumph of the human spirit. Outsiders helped, strangers reached out to them, but it is the falashas themselves—scorned and forgotten, obsessed by prophecy, stubborn in faith—who redeemed the dream.

I am indebted to the early scholars and researchers who

explored the history of these people, most especially to Wolf Leslau, who translated their ancient writings in his *Falasha Anthology,* and to David Kessler, Dr. G. J. Abbink, and Dr. Michele Schoenberger. I am grateful to other researchers and reporters who helped to break this story, including Tudor Parfitt of the University of London, Charles T. Powers of the *Los Angeles Times,* and Louis Rapoport of the *Jerusalem Post.* I also want to thank Shoshana Ben-Dor, the Jerusalem ethnologist, and Dr. Steven Kaplan of Hebrew University for sharing their insights.

I am grateful to Kenneth O. Gilmore, editor-in-chief of *Reader's Digest,* and Michael Blow, assistant managing editor, for their encouragement and generous help in developing this book. And I thank my agent, Don Congdon, and my editor at Prentice Hall Press, Paul D. Aron, for believing in it and seeing it through.

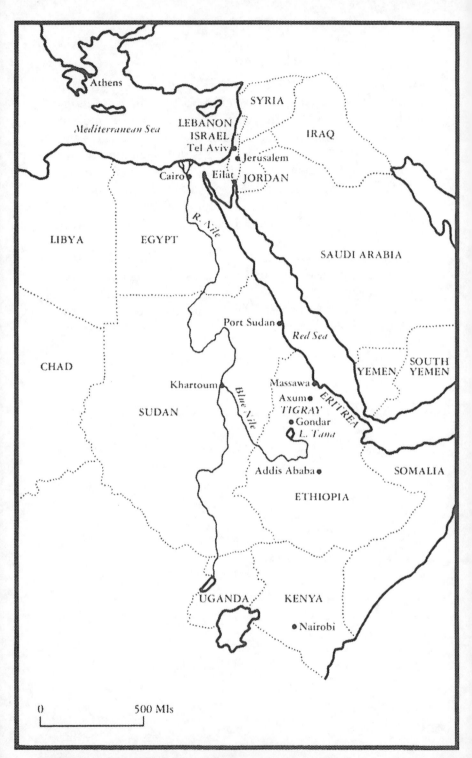

Courtesy of the author

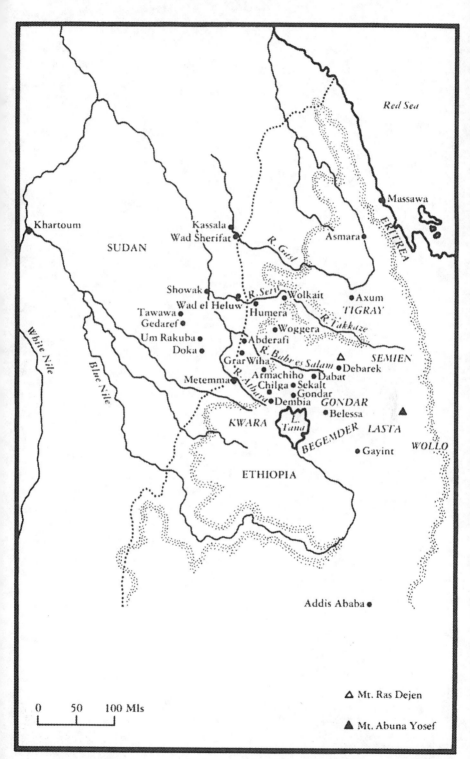

Courtesy of the author

*And it shall come to pass in that day,*
*That the Lord shall set His hand again a second time*
*To recover the remnant of His people,*
*Which shall be left, from Assyria, and from Egypt,*
*And from Pathros, and from Cush [Ethiopia] . . .*
*And there shall be an highway for the*
*remnant of His people . . .*
*Like as it was to Israel*
*In the day that he came up out of the land*
*of Egypt.*

—The Prophecy of Isaiah 11:11,16

*Do not separate me, O Lord,*
*from the chosen, from the joy,*
*from the light and the splendor.*
*Let me see, O Lord, the light of Israel,*
*and let me listen to the words of the just . . .*

—An old falasha prayer

# Chapter 1

# The Exodus Begins

A CONVOY of four buses, ancient and battered, emerges from the midnight shadows. For an uncertain moment, the buses pause. They have reached a remote strip at the edge of the airport, just outside of Khartoum, a historic crossroad for East and West, the fabled capital of Sudan.

A motor wheezes, a dinosaur catching its breath. Then the buses, covered with the dust of a race against time, lumber across the tarmac to the waiting plane.

Sudanese security officers have fanned out, guarding the scene, watching carefully. The ambassador from the United States, F. Hume Horan, has parked his car nearby, and he, too, is watching. It is December 1984, and he is sweating.

Even in winter, at this midsection of the world, it swelters in the Sudan. Today the temperature may climb to 100 degrees Fahrenheit. Yet it is not the weather that disturbs the ambassador's calm. It is life and death.

Under the pale moon that still hangs in the sky, who else has been watching? The buses are riding low, weighted down with this night's ragged cargo, a huddled mass of 220 men, women, and children. Some are sick, many are barefoot, all are dazed by their midnight ride.

These are people who have lived for months, and some of them for years, among the other homeless and hopeless in Sudan's refugee camps. Before that, they had made the long, desperate march out of Ethiopia, in flight from famine, civil wars, and the political and religious oppression of a Marxist military government.

In their Ethiopian villages, clusters of mud-and-straw huts, they were known as *Falashas,* an Ethiopian word that means wanderers or strangers. They call themselves *Beta Israel,* the House of Israel, the lost tribe of black Jews of Ethiopia, tattered but stubborn believers in the Old Testament prophecy that one day they would return to Jerusalem.

To Ambassador Horan, they are people in distress, refugees who need his help.

Every dawn for almost a month now, a plane has waited in the shadows for the buses to arrive. The flight plan lists a European capital as the plane's destination. Eventually, as the ambassador knows, these people will land in Israel, and he cannot help but worry.

How many more buses will make the trip, without being halted on the road? How many more planes will be allowed to come and quickly go? How many more lives can he and his secret partners save before the news gets out?

Among the first people out of the buses is a gaunt woman named Malka Alemie. Until she and her family began this odyssey, eight months earlier, she had never been more than twenty miles from her native village in the remote Wozago region of Gondar province in Ethiopia. She has never used an electric light, a telephone, or a pen and paper. She has never seen a flight of stairs such as she is now climbing.

At the end, she finds herself in an amazing place. So many chairs, she marvels, blinking at the rows and rows of passenger seats. Such a nice house. Nervously, she wonders, But where is the airplane?

Operation Moses was under way. It had been a long journey to this shadowy airstrip. Some people measured the trip in miles; others counted it in years.

Malka Alemie had yearned for this exodus all of her life. We are on the way now, she thought. The flying house shuddered and lifted off. It is happening. She felt herself being carried through the night skies, a simple woman in a prophetic dream.

*"And it shall come to pass in that day,"* it was written in Isaiah, *"that the Lord shall set His hand again a second time, to recover the remnant of His people, which shall be left, from Assyria, and from Egypt, and from Pathros, and from Cush [Ethiopia]* . . .

*"And there shall be an highway for the remnant of His people . . . like as it was to Israel in the day that he came up out of the land of Egypt."* (Isa. 11:11,16)

Malka sat straight-backed, wrapped in stillness, only her dark eyes darting everywhere, still watchful. It is safe now, she promised herself. She caught her reflection in the plane window. She was still a handsome woman, with even features and a proud head, like a bronze sculpture, but there were new lines there, carved in the last few months.

She closed her eyes, remembering. From the first step out of their Ethiopian village, she had known that her family was following a dangerous dream. Where is my husband? she thought now. Where are my daughters?

She remembered someone else—the bony young stranger who led her along the way to freedom. And Gideon? she wondered. Where is he?

# Chapter 2

# "The Time Is Now"

ETHIOPIA SITS, alone and mysterious, a fortress of craggy mountains in the eastern bulge of Africa. On its northern and western borders lies Sudan, and beyond that vastness there is Egypt. To the east is the Red Sea, separating Ethiopia from the Arabian Peninsula, flowing north until its waters touch the southern beaches of Israel and then run on to Suez.

The 490 falasha villages were scattered like chaff through the provinces of Gondar and Tigray in the northeast corner of Ethiopia. They were tossed among the farmlands of the Lake Tana region, where the Blue Nile begins, or perched among the peaks and crannies of the Semien Mountains.

Here, a dozen families in one village, two dozen in another, the poorest of the poor in Ethiopia struggled for survival. They were the remnant of a community that had once numbered a million. Over the centuries, their kings had been overthrown. Wars, disease, and conversions had decimated their numbers.

Mysterious and forgotten, a remnant endured. In 1862, when there may have been two hundred thousand of them left, a falasha named Abba Sagga sent a letter to "the chief priest of

4

all the Jews" in Jerusalem. "Has the time come," he asked, "that we should return to you, to our city, the holy city of Jerusalem?" There was no answer, but the address was vague, and the letter may never have been delivered.

A century later, they were dwindling again. They scratched out an existence among the Amharas, the dominant Coptic Christian majority of Ethiopia. A few of their neighbors were Moslems, the country's largest minority. Now they were living under siege, caught in the crossfire of revolution and civil war, trapped by drought and famine.

"If you will not help us quickly," a falasha leader wrote to the World Jewish Congress in 1973, "it is plain for everybody that we will not be anymore in this world."

Again there was no answer and no quick help. By 1980 there were fewer than twenty-eight thousand falashas alive in Ethiopia, a bare fraction of a percent of the country's population of 30 million.

Then, in the autumn of 1980, a letter came to a village of Woggera. Its *tukuls,* or huts—round frames of woven twigs and branches, plastered over with mud, covered with straw, topped with a pointed, overhanging straw roof—were huddled on a hillside. One hut flaunted the status symbol of African villages, a roof of corrugated iron.

Any Ethiopian could tell that this was a Jewish village. "You can smell them," a Coptic Christian told me. Because of their endless purification rituals, the Beta Israel are said to "smell of water."

There were other clues. No Star of David hung over the largest hut, the house of prayer, and there were no mezuzahs on the entrances of the others. But rows of pottery jars were baking in the sun in front of one hut; a weaver's loom stood in front of another; a lean-to sheltered the blacksmith's forge of still another. In this country, such crafts were despised; honor and status belonged to those who owned land. In this country, the Jews were the outcasts—the landless craftsmen.

The arrival of the letter was an event in this dozing, time-forgotten village, and its reading, over and over again, became a ritual. Presiding over it was Gideon, just eighteen years old, tall and bony, with the handsome, elongated face, straight nose, and large, dark eyes of Ethiopia.

The letter would change his life, but it wasn't addressed to Gideon. It had been written to a neighbor, a woman whose son had disappeared from the village a year earlier. Each month the anxious mother had made her way to the post office, a day's walk to another, larger town, hoping for word of him. Finally the letter came, but, like most Ethiopians—perhaps 90 percent of them, Jews, Christians, or Moslems—the woman couldn't read. She carried the paper as if it were gold leaf to Gideon, a village marvel, a young man with almost twelve years of schooling. "Please," she asked.

Again and again, Gideon read the letter for her. Its folds were tearing from so much reading. *"I have arrived in Jerusalem . . ."* the missing son wrote.

Each time he read the words, Gideon shivered. He thought of his people as "prisoners of the Torah," but now this letter writer had escaped the bonds of Ethiopia. As Gideon knew, other young men were also "disappearing," walking away in the night to fulfill an ancient prophecy.

Unlike any other Jews, the falashas had lost the Hebrew language. Unlike other Jews, they did not know about the Talmud, the second holy text of the Jews, the collection of laws and rabbinical wisdom. With just the Torah—the five books of Moses—the falashas built a wall of laws that kept them strong and faithful, separate and different. As if the Torah were a fortress, they lived behind it, keeping apart from their neighbors, clinging to their faith despite insults and assaults.

The people memorized the laws they could not read, and they kept the Sabbath strictly. At midday on Friday, all work stopped. The women swept their huts, then went to the stream to bathe and perform a cleansing ceremony. Purified, they could now prepare the Sabbath food. Then the men gathered at the stream to perform their own bathing rites. When a man's shadow lengthened to twelve paces, all fires were extinguished and the Sabbath had begun.

At sunset they gathered in the village's largest *tukul,* the synagogue. They faced north, to Jerusalem, as the *kes,* or priest, led them in prayer. At dawn on Saturday they were back, the men assembled on one side, the women on the other. There were no seats, and they stood through the long hours of prayer. The men leaned on their walking sticks. At times they pounded the sticks on the dirt floor, to keep tempo with the *kes*'s chants or to emphasize their own amens.

After the prayers, it was a day for resting, visiting, and the major falasha entertainment, storytelling. The villagers gathered under an acacia tree, squatting on the ground. The women sat apart, just outside the circle of men.

Gideon's grandfather, white-haired, leathery with age, sat in the center. In his eightieth year, he remembered the old stories better than anyone. *Tala,* a potent home-brewed beer, would keep the stories flowing, and someone brought a jug of it. No one poured for himself; instead, each man filled and refilled his neighbor's cup. Then they waited for the familiar words.

"We came from Jerusalem," the old man began, "and one day we will return to Jerusalem." Jerusalem—where their ancestors had prayed at the holy temple—was their name for all of the promised land.

"We came on foot, through the Sudan." In a singsong voice, the grandfather continued. "We will return on foot, through the Sudan."

There was a sigh of pleasure at the well-known words. For generations old men had been telling this story, but now they had a special reason for believing it.

"The letter." The woman neighbor passed the precious envelope to Gideon. "Read it to us again."

By now Gideon knew the words by heart, and so did his

listeners. But he performed the ritual, slipping the letter carefully from the envelope, unfolding it slowly.

"The way was hard, but I reached to Sudan," the letter said. "I was sick and hungry there. Then our people helped me, and so I have arrived in Jerusalem. I have seen the tomb of King David. I have said a prayer for you at the old wall of the Temple."

With the coming of the letter, Gideon made a fateful decision. He had a pass, signed by the local peasant leader, that allowed him to walk to a different village, to study at the government school there. Now he stopped that daily trek. He hired out as a farm laborer, collecting the money he would need for his trip.

A few months later, he too was gone from Woggera. Slipping away in the night, dodging government police and armed bandits, he walked the forbidden roads to Sudan.

Trying to leave Ethiopia is a crime, and parents are responsible for such sins of their children. When the local police discovered that Gideon had left the village, they arrested his father. For failing to report his son's "disappearance" within twenty-four hours, the father was put in prison for three months.

He was not the only father to be punished. Other people, mostly young men and women, were following Gideon's road. Out of each village, two or three people at a time, they walked by night across the dangerous miles to Sudan. Here they waited, often for a year or two. They tried to hide themselves among the tens of thousands of other hungry and ragged people in the dusty towns and refugee camps of Sudan, many of them growing sick and dying there. This was their purgatory, a place to linger until strangers from America or Israel helped them to go farther on the road to Jerusalem.

Gideon lingered longer than anyone else. When the chance came to leave for Jerusalem, he stayed behind in Sudan. He had found a dangerous vocation, working for volunteer rescuers from America and then for Israeli secret agents. For four years he lived undercover, changing his identity like a shirt. He had urgent work to do, important messages to deliver, lives to save.

Early in 1984, Gideon came walking back to Ethiopia. Something extraordinary was about to happen.

It began with a message, delivered to hundreds of remote villages without electricity, phones, or newspapers. In just a few days, the word was passed, so quickly that some said it came as a murmur on the wind. Others heard it as a quick whisper in a dusty marketplace. "Get ready," they were told. "The time is now." Here and there swift messengers moved along the narrow roads, coming and going like night shadows. One or two of them were young men who had returned all the way from Jerusalem. Others had come back, like Gideon, from Sudan.

Gideon felt conspicuous. He wore the familiar Ethiopian clothes: short trousers, a thin shirt, and a *shamma,* the national toga, around his shoulders. But the Sudan sun, stronger, crueler than Ethiopia's, had blackened his skin, and he was darker than anyone he passed along the roads. If the local police spotted him, they would have to wonder what this young man had been up to.

In a small village in the Wozago area, the people stared at him. Gideon was twenty-two now, and it was becoming rare to see anyone of that age in the falasha villages these days.

"Where are your young people?" he asked. "Have they all gone to Dembia?"

Malka Alemie lowered her eyes at the question. Her husband, Rachamim, shifted nervously. They understood the messenger's code. *Dembia* was distant, sparsely populated, a place to lose yourself in. It was the falasha word for the real but forbidden destination, Jerusalem. One of their daughters had "gone to Dembia" with her husband, but the rest of the family, afraid of the long wait in the terrible refugee camps of Sudan, had stayed behind.

The voice of Ethiopia is soft and low; foreigners find it hard to catch the words. But even for an Ethiopian, Gideon was whispering now.

"I know, I know," he said. "They went to Sudan." Rachamim nodded in agreement. "They are not there anymore," Gideon told them. "They have all been taken to Jerusalem."

"How?" Rachamim asked.

"There are many roads and many ways," Gideon whispered. "I cannot talk about them."

"All of them have gone?" Rachamim asked. "My daughter, too?" It was a year since she'd left, and there'd been no word of her yet.

The messenger smiled. During the past four years there had always been about two thousand Jews in the Sudanese camps, but not always the same two thousand. "Slow by slow," as the falashas say, word had drifted back to the villages that a few Jews had been smuggled out of the camps and on to Jerusalem. Then a few more had followed, to wait their turn and suffer in the refugee camps. Now the waiting and the suffering should be over. Now, mysteriously, almost all of the Jews were gone from the camps of Sudan. In small groups, in secret ways, they had been taken to Jerusalem.

"The ones who follow them," Gideon promised, "will be taken too."

A stream of hungry refugees was moving toward Sudan, a tide of human misery but a cloak for the exodus of the Jews. Malka watched her husband's face. The messenger was telling them that the road was open, and she prayed that Rachamim would make the right decision for their family.

"You know that we came from Jerusalem," Gideon was saying.

"They say that we came from the north, through Sudan," Rachamim whispered. His eyes were shining, and Malka knew they would be going. "They say that we shall return that way."

*Now.* Early in 1984, that word flew from one person to

another. *The time is now.* In hundreds of isolated villages, they heard that the longed-for day had come.

They answered the message. Lost in time, these are a calm and quiet people. Like the unswerving needle of a compass, they had yearned for a land that lay to the north. Now, on their own, they set out to fulfill the prophecy.

As one person, they rose up. They had no general, no president, no leader, no governing body. Yet like a single soul on fire, twelve thousand men, women, and children marched out of those scattered villages and began a long and desperate journey.

The exodus was unplanned and unexpected. As they poured into the refugee camps of Sudan, they caught the governments of the world by surprise.

Israel had thought that a few hundred people, perhaps even a thousand, would answer the message. Her secret agents had ways of helping a few falashas at a time, but no plan for rescuing so many thousands.

Now Israel and her good friend, the United States, would have to devise a plan. It would be called Operation Moses— after the leader of the first exodus out of Egypt, the prophet who in his youth, according to Numbers 12:1, took an Ethiopian bride.

# Chapter 3

# The Road to Freedom

TZION ALEMIE, age three, watched the skies over the small village in the Wozago region. Once or twice a day there was a distant speck, a plane. He raced after it, barefoot, along the dirt paths and across the brown fields.

"Stop!" he shouted. "Wait for me! Take me to Jerusalem!"

"Ssh," his grandmother Malka warned him. "It's a secret. No one must know." After centuries of dreaming, generations of hoping, years of whispering, they were almost ready now.

Ever since the messenger's visit, they had been planning and preparing. It had been a lean harvest that year, and by mid-April the storage jars of grain were almost empty. The meals were skimpy—just some *injera,* the flat, spongy bread of Ethiopia, with a topping of *wot,* the fiercely peppered vegetable stew. It had been a long time since she put some meat in that stew. Still, from each day's meals Malka hoarded a bit of food for their trek: some grain, some dried chickpeas, and, most precious of all, some coffee beans.

"I came to this *tukul* as a bride," she remembered. She was almost sixty now, her hair still black, her smile still hopeful, her long, graceful hands still fluttering like excited birds when she talked. Two of her daughters had left the *tukul* as brides for other villages. Now they were back, with their husbands and children, crowding into the small space, about fifteen feet in diameter, waiting to make the trek with her.

"After all these years," Malka sighed, "we do not have many things." The hands swooped in a sudden nostalgia. Whatever they had, they were selling. The baskets she'd woven, her own designs, a geometry of color, were already gone. Her husband, Rachamim, a farmer and a blacksmith, had sold his plowshare and his tools. The land and the *tukul* were not theirs to sell, but Eigal, their married son, almost thirty now, was negotiating over their two oxen and the sheep.

"So you want to sell?" The buyer was a farmer from a neighboring Christian village. "Why?" he asked. "Why are you leaving?"

Eigal shrugged. The Ethiopian Jew and the Ethiopian Christian looked like brothers, with a historic family resemblance of large eyes, straight noses, and lean black bodies. As farmers, they lived alike, in the rhythm of the seasons.

"The dryness is coming," Eigal said.

It was true. It was spring, planting time, but the sky was cloudless and the fields around them were brown, hard, and dry. The wet season was supposed to begin soon, but the rains— heavy, constant, nourishing the land—had not come last year. The land had not turned its emerald green, the grain harvest had been pale and stunted, and cattle were lean and scrawny. "This year will be the same," Eigal predicted. "Maybe worse."

In good years these farmers scratched out a bare living. Ethiopians earned a per capita average of about $120 a year, but most falashas usually fell far below that small sum. In bad years like these, hunger gnawed at many people. The terrible drought that had struck Tigray and other parts of Ethiopia was edging closer to their province of Gondar, bringing famine with it.

Eigal did not talk of the other reasons—the old hatreds that were flaring again, the Marxist government that made him feel more of a falasha, more of a stranger, than ever. An American Jewish group had sent a Torah scroll for his village, but the local police had seized and burned it. The Jewish school where he'd hoped to send his children was shut down, its teachers arrested and tortured as "Zionist spies." For a while the governor of Gondar had ordered the village synagogue closed, and Eigal knew it could be shut again, for no reason, at any time. To himself, he mourned, They will not let us live as ourselves, as Jews.

He was obsessed with the Passover promise, "Next year in Jerusalem," but it was a forbidden dream. A month before, a young man had been stopped on the road, accused of trying to escape to Israel, and beaten on the soles of his feet. "So you will not run again," the police torturers had said, smirking. Eigal felt trapped. They don't want us here, he thought, and they don't want to let us go.

In silence, Eigal accepted the low prices. He always did. In normal times he went to market day in a nearby town to sell the plowshares and other metal tools that he and his father had forged. The Amharics, the local people, sought out the falasha metalcrafts. They thought the falashas were *buda,* or witches, with magic spells that made their tools strong and unbreakable. Yet they always offered low prices, and Eigal, knowing there would be insults if he asked for more, never haggled.

Today's buyer was friendlier, less superstitious than most. He didn't believe in the falasha "evil eye," and he looked Eigal full in the face. "I'm sorry you are going," he said. "Who will make my tools for me now?"

Finally they were ready. The day had come. Eigal and his mother looked across the fields at the distant hills. What lay beyond them?

For one last time, Malka carried the clay water jug to the spring. It weighed twenty pounds empty, but she shooed away the younger women who offered to help. Filled, it was heavy on her back as she carried it home. You will have to be as strong as those oxen we sold, she told herself.

For one last time, she lit the cooking fire in her *tukul*. She poured the yeasty flour-and-water mix for circles of *injera*. For one last time, her family gathered for a meal, sitting on the floor around a low woven-straw table.

The first circle of *injera* went to Rachamim. Murmuring a blessing, he tore off a piece for himself and then distributed pieces for everyone.

"For so long, our people waited for a deliverer," he said, "but nobody came to deliver us."

Malka smiled, nodding at her husband's words. "Now we will deliver ourselves."

They waited. Rachamim and Eigal loaded two mules with their sacks of food and jerrycans of water. Malka doused the last embers of the fire. "One minute more," she said. Before she abandoned it, she wanted to sweep the dirt floor of her *tukul*.

Then three generations of Alemies were ready to leave. With parents, children, grandchildren, and in-laws, there were twenty-seven of them to join the other families at the village edge.

They were simple people, thin shadows in the dark night, straight-backed, with a quiet dignity. Rachamim's legs showed out like bare sticks from under his short trousers and *shamma*. Malka had wrapped her head in a fringed cloth, and she wore her *kamise,* the traditional, ankle-length Ethiopian dress, loose-fitting and sashed at the waist. Her husband had woven the cloth for it, and she had sewn it by hand and embroidered the edges.

The tender blue of the sky turned trembling and dark. In a sudden moment, the sun dropped behind the horizon. Beneath the sheltering night sky, armed only with walking sticks, they began their exodus.

An entire village, about a hundred people, moved across the brown fields. Only half were leaving on this trip, but the others accompanied them for the first few miles. The road led to Sudan, and no one was sure what would happen after that. When it was time for the two groups to part, the villagers embraced and kissed one another, first on one cheek, then the other, three quick times. "We will meet again in Jerusalem," Malka promised an old friend who was staying behind.

The first miles were easy ones, a dirt path across the rolling countryside. The sun was rising again as they crossed a stretch of empty fields and reached the safety of a dense grove of trees. Here, they'd arranged to meet the Christian guides who knew the difficult roads to Sudan.

Gruff men were waiting for them, with automatic rifles, menacing Russian-made Kalashnikovs, slung over their shoulders. The guides were members of the *shifta,* the bandit gangs that roamed the countryside, hardened at eluding the police and soldiers along the roads.

Malka shivered. Her family's lives were now in the hands of armed bandits. Their leader stepped forward. "I am Josef of Armachiho." Rachamim reached under the folds of his *shamma* for a knotted bundle of money and paid him almost all they had—one hundred *birr* (Ethiopian currency, worth about fifty cents American) for each member of the family.

From other villages, others came. By nightfall they had grown into a huddled mass of three hundred people. Josef took their money and gave them their orders. They would walk by night and rest by day. They would not wait for stragglers. "Day and night, you must be quiet," he told them. "If a child cries, you must cover his mouth." Grimly, he warned, "If you make noise, it will bring the government troops. Then we will have to run away from you."

In the darkness, a hushed line of men, women, and children moved out. That first night, they moved across the farmlands and past the shadowy *tukuls* of an unknown village. Tree branches slapped at them, and stones bruised their legs. Then the road began to rise, leading them up a craggy hillside. At midnight, Malka was grateful for a brief rest. Then they were moving again, stopping only with the daylight.

"No fires here," the guides warned them. "It's too open." They ate the roasted peas and crackers they had brought with them. The children were dazed and frightened. "Eat, eat," Malka told them. "We are coming out of Egypt. These are our matzohs."

Wrapped in their *shammas,* they stretched out on the hard ground to rest. In the bright morning light, Malka shuddered. She brushed away the strange insects that were crawling over her makeshift pillow. She slapped at a creeping thing that was biting her leg. Then, exhausted, she fell asleep.

She awoke, her body stiff and aching. At sundown, it was time to move out again. Mile after mile, the road grew steeper. They leaned heavily on their walking sticks. When they rested, they drank the water sparingly. The guides knew where to find more water, but already some of the springs they counted on were dry.

In the dusk of the third day, Malka woke to sounds of confusion. "Too many people," she heard one of the guides say. "Too easy to be caught." Two smaller groups could move more quickly, more invisibly, than one endless caravan.

Suddenly, the guides were pulling at people, dividing them into two groups. "Quickly, quickly," the guides ordered. "You go there. And you come here."

In the dim light, in the guides' haste, families were separated. One of the guides shrugged. "Maybe you will find each other in Sudan." Half the group, about 150 people, were led away to follow a different route to the border. The other half were being pushed into a line to follow Josef and his remaining men.

In the gathering darkness, Malka searched frantically up and down the line of bewildered people who remained. "My husband? Have you seen my husband?" She could not find him. "Eigal," she called, "where are your sisters?" Her son shook his head. They were gone too. His wife, Kohava, was crying; her parents had been traveling with them, and now they too were missing. Rachamim, two daughters, their husbands and children, the in-laws—all together, nineteen members of the family were gone, pulled away by the guides to follow a separate road to Sudan.

Blindly, Malka followed the steep trail of her own caravan. She had been walking for four hours when she thought she heard gunfire, the echo of rifle shots off in the distance.

She stopped, peering into the black night, searching for her lost family. She shivered with a terrible premonition, but there was nothing to see and nothing more to hear. What was happening? The line of weary marchers kept moving past her. "Don't fall behind, mama," a guide warned her.

When they stopped at dawn, she was calm. She shared her foreboding with no one. All her life Malka had been dutiful, first to her father and then to her husband. She had been loving, hard-working, and silent for them. Now there was no man to speak for her.

There is no time for tears, she told herself. Now she had to find her own voice. Her new duty was to be head of the family that remained. She had to be a *baaltet,* "a wise mother" to whom others, men as well as women, would listen.

Hidden among the rocks and trees that day, they lit a cooking fire. With coffee to drink, she felt stronger. "No one else must be lost," she instructed her family. "Resting or walking, we must stay close together."

There were just eight of them left. Malka put the daughter who remained, teenaged Mazel, in charge of grandson Avi, age nine, frightened and weeping for the mother who had been pulled away with the other group. Her son, Eigal, led the mule that carried little Tzion and his five-year-old sister, Orit. His wife, Kohava, carried their other child, a dozing infant held on her back in an *ankelba,* a baby sack made of leather and worn like a backward apron.

Malka walked behind them. She did not want them watching and worrying when her body slumped with fatigue and her feet dragged. They were moving across the Ethiopian plateau, climbing its steep and stony ridges.

In the darkness, Malka stumbled against a sharp rock. The pain left her breathless. Clapping a hand over her mouth, she would not let herself cry out. She could feel warm, sticky blood pouring down her leg. Quickly, she tore a strip of cloth from her *shamma* and wrapped the wound. Limping, with the wound festering and throbbing, she struggled to keep the silhouettes of her family in sight.

Two nights later, the gunshots were close by. "Down!" the guides shouted. "Get down!" Malka had never been under fire before, but she acted on instinct. She grabbed for one of her grandchildren, pulling little Tzion from the mule, covering the child with her own body. Her son, Eigal, flung himself on top of young Orit.

More shots rang out. Ethiopia was in turmoil, and it could have been anybody's finger on the trigger. Government troops no longer controlled this area or the border, but they ran patrols here. So did insurgents from Tigray. Fighting for independence from Ethiopia, rebel troops from Eritrea province sometimes roamed this far. So did other armed bands still loyal to the fallen emperor, Haile Selassie.

This time it was *shifta,* another group of bandits demanding money to allow the caravan to pass. Their guides, bandits too, were firing back. Malka pressed herself and the child close to the ground. She could hear other children crying. A mule skittered down the stony mountain, taking a precious load of water with him. The shooting seemed to go on for a long time.

Finally it stopped. Now the shouting started. Malka whispered a warning to Eigal. "Watch the guides closely." She knew that some guides betrayed their people. Some led them straight to government troops. Other guides disappeared after a few days, leaving the people stranded on an unknown road.

In an ambush like this one, most guides let the other *shifta* stop the caravan and go from person to person, collecting money. If someone had no money to give, the bandits took a mule, the last sack of food, or the person's only pair of sandals. Sometimes the ambush was really a rendezvous, and the two groups of bandits met later to divide the booty.

The bandits were negotiating. "You cannot take money from these poor people," Josef, the guide leader, shouted. "They have paid me, and from that money I will pay you." He paused and fired a shot in the air. "But only a little."

When they settled on a sum, the caravan moved on. Malka remembered the young messenger, Gideon, who had sent them to this guide. "He was right," she whispered to Eigal. "Our bandit is an honest one."

The road grew steeper and narrower. In the darkness they walked single file, aware that a misstep would take them over the edge of a deep precipice. Gasping for breath, hot with fever from the throbbing wound on her leg, Malka hugged the mountain wall.

When the road widened again, the guides signaled a halt. They could rest here briefly. Other people had followed this road before them; tens of thousands of Ethiopians—Christians, Moslems, and Jews—were fleeing the famine and political turmoil. For many miles now, Malka had seen the things those other people had thrown away to lighten their load. Empty water jugs. Sacks that had once held food. Worn-out sandals.

Now, in the moonlight, Malka saw something else. An *ankelba*. The young mother, Kohava, saw it too, and knew. A woman would throw away her baby carrier only if the baby had died. Kohava reached for the *ankelba* on her own back, stroking the sleeping infant within.

Now it was she who had a foreboding. Seeing the terror on

Kohava's face, Malka tried to calm her. "No, no," she said, "it won't happen."

Yet when they began again, Malka was remembering the rest of the grandfathers' prophecy.

*"The way will be hard,"* they had always said. *"Not everyone will arrive."*

## Chapter 4

# Wanderers and Warriors

WHO ARE THEY, these dark-skinned wanderers? Where do they come from? Alone and forgotten for two millenniums, how did they survive?

The falashas' own answers are in myths and legends, an oral history told around the fires from one generation to another. Their written records were lost in the turbulent centuries.

In the written records of other people, there are scattered hints. Scholars have found the first references to Jews in Ethiopia in Greek writings two hundred years before Christ. In the ninth century A.D., Eldad ha-Dani, a traveler who may have been a falasha himself, reported that one of the ten lost tribes had survived in the remote Semien Mountains of Ethiopia.

In the twelfth century, another Jewish traveler, a Spanish merchant named Benjamin of Tudela, brought back an account of an independent Jewish kingdom in Ethiopia. Three hundred years later, Elia of Ferrara, an Italian scholar living in the Holy Land, wrote of meeting a falasha in Jerusalem, a young man who told him of the "continual wars" his people fought with the Coptic emperors of Ethiopia.

"We came from Solomon," the falashas used to explain. The biblical story of King Solomon and Queen Sheba is brief, a few lines telling of the queen's visit to Jerusalem, bearing gifts for the famous king and asking questions about his God.

For the Ethiopians, it is a royal romance, told in rich detail down the centuries, the subject of comic-strip-like drawings that are still sold on the bustling streets of the capital city, Addis Ababa. The story is the heart of the national saga of Ethiopia, the *Kebra Nagast* or "Glory of Kings."

In this epic, Sheba made the long and difficult trip to Jerusalem with a caravan of camels, loaded with rare spices, gold, and precious jewels. She questioned the King of Israel about his God, and his answers made a convert of her. "From this moment," she told Solomon, "I will not worship the sun but will worship the creator of the sun, the God of Israel. And that Tabernacle of the God of Israel shall be unto me my Lady, and unto my seed after me. . . ."

Solomon, according to this epic, was wily, with earthly pleasures on his mind, and he tricked the beautiful queen into his bed. Nine months later, back in Ethiopia, she gave birth to a child whom she named Menelik, "son of the wise man."

Emperor Haile Selassie, "the Lion of Judah," was the last of a long line of Ethiopian rulers who claimed to be the heirs of that child. In Europe, kings ruled by "divine right"; in Ethiopia, they claimed the throne as direct descendants of the ancient kings of Israel. If they were related to Solomon, the son of King David, that also made them kin to the founder of Christianity, Jesus of Nazareth.

In 1936, when Selassie was in exile, he found himself at a formal dinner in Cambridge, England. Abba Eban, who would eventually become one of the leaders of the new state of Israel, was among the other guests. "Very interesting legend about Solomon and the Queen of Sheba," Eban remarked. The banished king stiffened. "It is not a legend," he answered, deeply offended. "It is a fact."

When Menelik was grown, the *Kebra Nagast* relates, he retraced his mother's road to Jerusalem. He visited his father and saw the great temple that Solomon had built to house the Ark of the Covenant, the gold-encrusted chest that held the tablets of the Ten Commandments handed down on Mount Sinai.

In revenge for Solomon's seduction of Sheba, Menelik then stole the Ark and brought it to the city of Axum, Ethiopia's ancient northern capital. Here he planned to establish "the new Zion." The Ark has disappeared in the mists of time. According to one legend, it was hidden during one of Ethiopia's many civil wars and never found again.

The falashas used to cherish bits and pieces of this national epic, and they had one of their own. According to this story, an elite guard of Hebrew soldiers escorted Menelik home to Ethiopia, the biblical land of Cush and Abyssinia. On a Friday evening, the followers of Menelik arrived at the mythical river of Sambatyon. (For the falashas, the Sambatyon may have been a reference to the rushing waters of the Blue Nile. In wider Jewish folklore, it is a river that exists on no map; it is said to swirl and run swiftly, except on the Sabbath, when it rests and is calm.) Those who continued the journey, crossing the Sambatyon, eventually became Ethiopian Christians; those who paused at the river, keeping the Sabbath, remained Jews and were the ancestors of the falashas.

In recent decades, tourists who came to see Lake Tana, the source of the Blue Nile, also stopped at one or two falasha villages to gawk at the phenomenon of black Jews. To earn money, the falasha women made and sold clay figurines of Solomon and Sheba, usually embracing in a little clay nuptial bed.

Yet they no longer believed that story. Slowly, as the outside world reached into their isolated villages, they heard and adopted other stories.

"We come from Dan," the Beta Israel say today. Other Jews

first accepted them as brothers in the sixteenth century, when the revered Radbaz, the great Rabbi David Ben Zimra of Cairo, decreed, "It is clear that they are the seed of Israel, of the tribe of Dan, which dwells in the mountains of Ethiopia." In 1973, when the chief rabbis of modern Israel recognized them as true Jews, it was as the remnant of that lost tribe of Dan, one of the ten tribes of Israel captured by the Assyrians in 722 B.C. and then vanished in history.

Lost tribe or not, that's a mystery of faith. Historically, before the rise of the Cross and then the Crescent, the religion of Judaism had spread far and wide. Carried by travelers and traders, soldiers and settlers, it had reached the countries of the Mediterranean and spread along the Red Sea.

Wherever they went, the Jews brought their ethical teachings and their concept of one God. They won many converts, so that there were 8 million Jews in the known world by the first century B.C. It was not until much later, when the Jewish community closed ranks to protect itself, that proselytizing was discouraged by the rabbis.

All through Jewish history, there has been a diaspora. A hundred years before Jesus was born, according to some scholars, there were three times as many Jews living outside the Holy Land as within its borders.

Among these far-flung colonies were a number of ancient settlements in Egypt. There was a large Jewish community in Alexandria. There were Jewish soldiers and ivory traders on Elephantine Island in the Nile River, near where Aswan stands today. By some accounts, the Elephantine soldiers were descendants of the warrior tribe of Dan. On their island they had built a temple the size of Solomon's Temple in Jerusalem. Their letters and papers have been found recently and translated.

In times of trouble, such as a rebellion at the Elephantine garrison, these Jews trekked south through Sudan and eventually arrived in the highlands of Ethiopia. There they found green mountains, a temperate climate, and a native people, the

Agau, whom they converted to Judaism and whose women they married.

Other Jews—travelers, traders, and even prisoners of war from across the Red Sea in Western Arabia and Yemen—may have joined them. Indeed, some scholars think that the Arabian Jews may have settled in Ethiopia even before their Egyptian brothers.

Whoever came first, they flourished. Half of Ethiopia, according to national legend, was Jewish until the fourth century A.D., when the country was converted to Christianity by King Ezana. One of that king's gold coins, dropped from the pocket of an early pilgrim, was found recently in the ruins of an ancient church in Jerusalem.

In those early centuries, the falashas were an independent people. The history of this time is a mix of legends, lightly salted with facts. In this era they lived mostly in the Semien Mountains, whose rocks and precipices formed a series of natural fortresses. Here they were ruled by a line of kings called Gideon and queens called Judith. Sporadically, they fought bloody wars with their neighbors.

Late in the tenth century, they were led by a warrior queen. By falasha legend, this Queen Judith was "as beautiful as Sheba." In Hebrew, her name was Jehudit. In ancient Ge'ez, the language Ethiopians still use for their prayers, *yehudit* means "very beautiful."

Judith is said to have cut a swath from the Red Sea port of Massawa to the ancient capital of Axum, gathering soldiers as she went and conquering everything in her path. The Moslems had just overthrown the Christian rulers of Egypt, and Judith may have been hoping to lead the Jews to the same triumph in Ethiopia.

At Axum she was victorious again, leveling the city, destroying its palaces and churches. Only the Ark of the Covenant, removed for safekeeping before her attack, escaped her.

"The lands are abandoned without a shepherd," the embattled Amharic ruler wrote to the Christian king of Nubia. "Our bishops and priest are dead, and the churches are ruined." For the next forty years, Queen Judith ruled over northern Ethiopia.

Some historians suspect that Judith was just a legend, but Ethiopians believe in her as gospel. The falashas treasure her victories, telling stories of Judith to each new generation of wide-eyed children. The Amharas retell the stories, too, remembering Judith as "the bloodthirsty queen" and "the whore of Axum." She is supposed to have led her armies into battle in A.D. 975; almost a thousand years later, when the Amharic Christians attacked the village of Wollo in 1972 and killed thirty falashas, they claimed the bloodletting was revenge for "the whore of Axum."

No one knows whether the Jews were black, brown, or white when they first arrived in "the land of the burnt faces," as the Greeks named Ethiopia. Indeed, as Malka Alemie asks today, "Do you know about our father Abraham? Was he black or white?"

Behind her mountains, Ethiopia was unlike her African neighbors, and anthropologists classify her people as Caucasian rather than Negroid. "We are dark, the color of the earth of Ethiopia," Malka Alemie explained. "In Israel, the earth is white and so are the people." (When the first falashas were airlifted to Israel, some of the women wondered whether their babies born there would be white.)

The events that Jews around the world celebrate at Purim and Hanukkah—and the events that Christians celebrate at Christmas and Easter—had not yet taken place when Malka's ancestors arrived in Ethiopia. The Talmud, the laws and commentaries that govern Jewish life, had not yet been written. The falashas arrived in Ethiopia with only the Torah, the first five books of Moses.

In this mountain fastness, they kept their faith and Jewish identity for two millenniums. In the confusion of centuries, unlike any other Jewish community—even the far-flung Chinese Jews of Kaifeng-Fu and the Cochin Jews of India—the Ethiopians lost the Hebrew language. Their *Orit,* or Torah, was written on the parchment pages of a book, rather than on the traditional scrolls of other Jews.

Cut off from the outside world, they were unaware of the changes other Jews had made. Like the Jews of the Temple era, they still had animal sacrifices and they still called their religious leaders *kesoch,* or priests, instead of rabbis or teachers. They had no yarmulkas, or skullcaps, and only the priest wore a white turban to cover his head.

As if it were a jewel, they guarded their Jewish identity, living apart from their gentile neighbors. Jews in many countries have been accused of being stubborn, stiff-necked, and clannish, and nowhere was this more obvious or more exaggerated than among the falashas. It was a survival technique, a way of warding off their worst fears—assimilation, intermarriage, and conversion, forced or voluntary.

Their religious laws were strict, and many of their customs and rituals seemed especially designed to keep them different and apart. Because of their dietary rules, for example, they were forbidden to eat food prepared by a nonfalasha.

They struggled to survive as a community, living in their villages as if under siege, clinging to their faith despite the insults and assaults of their neighbors. A falasha village always had to be close to a stream or lake, so that they could perform their endless cleansing rituals. There were elaborate purification rites for the Sabbath and every holiday. Until recently, most falashas went through a cleansing ceremony after any contact, even the most casual meeting, with an "unclean" person, meaning a nonfalasha.

They read the Torah literally. Other religious Jews consider it "nonkosher" to eat meat and dairy products together, because of the biblical injunction "Thou shalt not seethe a kid in its mother's milk." The falashas interpreted this more narrowly, as a ban against eating the calf with cow's milk, but not with goat's milk.

Unlike other Jews, the falashas isolated their women at certain times. In every family compound of *tukuls* there was a special hut, "the house of blood," where women lived apart during their menstrual periods. As Deuteronomy specifies, the women also were isolated for forty days after they'd given birth to a boy and eighty days after a girl.

Malka Alemie cannot remember any woman ever objecting to this. Along with cooking and caring for the children, women's work was hauling water, carrying wood, threshing, and grinding grain. Recalling that, her hands fly to her face, hiding a smile. "The hut," she insists, "was our vacation."

Ethiopian Jews and Christians speak the same modern Semitic language, Amharic, and pray in the same ancient tongue, Ge'ez, often with the same words and melodies. Both circumcise their sons on the eighth day. They share many of the same dietary laws, including the ban on pork.

Once the falashas had monks. These were their most learned men, celibate hermits who trained their priests. By tradition, these monks were originally Christians who left the Ethiopian church in a fifteenth-century schism over how "Jewish" it should be. They moved north to join with the falashas, and had a strong influence on their religion, especially on the liturgy. As some elderly falashas used to say, "The monks brought us our prayers."

To this day, the Copts of Ethiopia have more Judaic elements in their religion than other Christian churches. Once, they kept the Sabbath on Saturday. Until recently, the Star of David was more of a Christian symbol than a Jewish one in Ethiopia. Even now, almost every Ethiopian church has a prominent Star of David and a conspicuous replica of the tablets of Moses.

Jews and Christians should have lived in Ethiopia like brothers, and they did—Cain and Abel. Endlessly, they fought each other. The bloodiest era lasted almost four centuries, "the Period of the Wars" from 1270 to 1632.

Like most wars, these were about land and power, but they were also a sibling rivalry, a struggle over a heavenly father's love. The Jews claimed a covenant with God as "the chosen people." As the heirs of Menelik and the founders of "the new Zion," the Ethiopian Christians believed they had become "God's chosen," and their battles against the Jews had the hot zeal of a crusade.

Over and over, the falashas rebelled. Again and again, they were conquered. With each defeat, more and more of them were pushed out of their Semien strongholds and onto the plains of Gondar province.

In 1415, when the falashas rose again, they were put down by King Ishaq. He ordered the Jews to convert and issued a decree: "He who is baptized in the Christian faith may inherit the land of his fathers; otherwise, let him be a *Falassi.*"

With that, the Jews became strangers in Ethiopia, rootless and landless. The decree is the oldest written reference to *falassi,* an ancient Ge'ez word that in time became *falasha* in the modern language of Ethiopia, Amharic. Ironically, the original copy of the decree was lost for three hundred years, then rediscovered in modern times by a falasha, Tadessa Yacob.

Five years after King Ishaq's reign, bloodied but still fierce, the falashas revolted once more. This time they were defeated by King Zara Yacob, who proudly took the title of "exterminator of the Jews."

One violent struggle followed another. In the fifteenth century, defeated in battle and ordered to convert to Christianity, some Ethiopian Jews had to practice their religion in secret, like the marranos in Spain. Others continued to hold out in their mountain fortresses, independent but impoverished. In sixteenth-century writings, there is an account of an Ethiopian king who took a royal prisoner, a falasha king. "He was not very rich," the Ethiopian scoffed. "The king of the falashas had to plow his own fields."

In the late sixteenth century, King Sarsa Dengel launched a military campaign to crush the "infidels." By then the first Europeans, the Portuguese, had arrived in Ethiopia, bringing guns to help their new friends fight first the Moslems and then the Jews. Against the king's firepower the falashas had only spears and shields. One by one, their Semien fortresses fell.

Gideon, the bony messenger of our story, comes from the region of Woggera, where the last mountain stronghold of the Jews was besieged. To escape a fatal choice, conversion or slavery, many of them leaped to their deaths. *"Adonai,"* they cried to God with their last breaths, "help me." Like the zealots of Masada, others killed each other with swords and spears till no one was left alive.

With that, armed rebellion ended. For two centuries the falashas were forgotten by history. Then, in 1770, Ethiopians were startled by a red-bearded giant who appeared in their midst, searching, he explained, for the source of the Blue Nile. Along the way, James Bruce, the famous Scottish explorer, rediscovered the falashas.

On his route to Lake Tana, traveling through the Semien Mountains and the province of Gondar, Bruce noted that the area "is in great part possessed by Jews." His account of their life then, wretched and impoverished, would still be true two hundred years later for Malka Alemie and her family. "These are the ancient inhabitants of the mountains who still preserve the religion, language and manners of their ancestors, and live in villages by themselves," Bruce wrote in *Travels to Discover the Source of the Nile.* "Their number is now considerably diminished, and this has proportionally lowered their power and spirit. They are now wholly addicted to agriculture, hewers of wood and carriers of water, and the only potters and masons in Abyssinia."

In Europe, the Christian missionary movement was gathering steam and passion. They read Bruce's report of a forgotten community of Jews in Ethiopia, and they paid more attention to it than the Jews of the world did. Seized by the idea of converting a lost tribe of Jews, an army of missionaries descended on the falasha villages. They came from all branches of Christianity, and nothing dampened their ardor, not even the Ethiopian decree that all converts had to be baptized in the Coptic church. To the European missionaries, that was less than ideal, but it was a start.

The missionaries preached a message of a messiah who had come to Jerusalem long ago and been accepted by many of the Jews. "In your ignorance," they told the falashas, "in your isolation, you did not hear about it."

It was not a new message for the falashas, but it came at a curious time. The Jews knew of the Ethiopian Christian tradition—that when the messiah returned he would be called Theodore ("beloved of God"). In 1862 the emperor of Ethiopia took that name, Theodore, and announced he was that savior. The falasha villagers were confused. Had the day finally come?

Long before Malka Alemie's trek, a yearning multitude of black Jews rose up out of their villages. Obsessed by redemption, dizzy with messiah talk, drunk on prophecy, singing songs, thousands of them began a march to Jerusalem. All they knew was the general direction—north. They hoped for the same miracles that brought Moses out of Egypt. For three years they wandered, many of them dying of starvation and disease. Some settled in new villages in Tigray; a few survivors returned to their ruined homes in Gondar province; none reached Jerusalem.

They picked up their lives as serfs, working the poorest plots of ground and turning one-third to one-half of their crops over to the landlord. They survived by using their traditional skills as blacksmiths, weavers, and potters. At any time the Jewish tenant could be evicted from the land, and it was rare that a falasha family managed to farm the same plot of ground for more than three generations.

When their Amharic neighbors looked at the Jews they saw their worst nightmares—being without land, being despised craftsmen—in living flesh. To ward off those evils, their neighbors accused the Jews of being *buda,* or witches, creatures who turned into hyenas at night, and of devouring children. In their own self-defense and superstition, the falashas believed they must avoid being touched by "unclean" gentiles.

In 1867, for a brief moment, the Jews of Europe took notice of their brothers and sisters in Ethiopia. Alarmed by news of the Christian missionaries, they sent one of their own, a French scholar named Joseph Halévy.

Arriving at the falasha villages, Halévy held out a hand in friendship. "I am a white falasha," he told them, but they were skeptical. The missionaries, including some converted Jews, often used that phrase. "I am a Jew," Halévy tried again, but the falashas only stared. They knew Ethiopian terms like *Ayud* and *Kayla,* insulting, contemptuous words, but this lost tribe had never heard the word *Jew.*

"I am from the House of Israel," Halévy said. This was their name, the Beta Israel. They recognized him as one of their own, and they wept. In their long exile, they had thought they were the only Jews left in the world. They had not imagined that there could be Jews with white skins.

Halévy returned to Europe, hoping to stir interest in the falashas. He argued with Jewish leaders, spoke to any group who would listen, and wrote articles and books on the desperate plight of the falashas. He wrote:

The Falasha harnesses himself to the plow with his wife and children in order not to die of hunger. Fearing that he will not harvest what he has sown, he abandons his field and attempts to gain a livelihood by handicraft which brings in little. . . . He visits the markets but he will be fortunate if, on his return, he is not robbed by the soldiers or the outlaws who infest the highways. He returns home as poor, but more miserable than before, bringing back nothing for his children except a fatherly kiss.

For the Jews of Europe, the idea of a lost tribe of black Jews in Ethiopia was too remote, too strange. Halévy had brought a falasha back with him, to be educated as a teacher for his people. The Europeans stared at this living proof of a lost tribe. Some of them suspected that the young man was not a black Jew at all but a slave whom Halévy had bought in the markets of Sudan. The young man died before he could return to his family in Ethiopia.

For the white Jews who listened to Halévy or read his books, there were questions. Were these people Jews? Or "almost Jews"? Or something other than Jews?

No other religion would ask those questions. If someone says he is Catholic, Lutheran, Moslem, almost anything, if he accepts the teachings and follows the laws of that religion, that is usually that. Yet Judaism is different. The debate over those questions lasted a hundred years, and the answers came slowly and stingily.

The falashas had not asked for money, machinery, or other material comforts. They yearned for education, for a link with the Jews of the world, for a sign they were no longer alone. Yet Halévy's pleas on behalf of the falashas fell mostly on deaf ears.

Halévy was an old man, a graying professor at the Sorbonne in Paris, when he found a rapt listener. A young student, a rabbi's son from Lodz, Poland, was inspired by the stories of the mysterious falashas. Finally, in 1904, Jacques Faitlovitch followed his teacher's footsteps to Ethiopia.

## Chapter 5

# *No Longer Alone*

FOUR DECADES HAD passed since Halévy's visit, with no word. Some of the falashas thought the visit must have been a dream. Others mourned the silence.

Then, in 1904, Jacques Faitlovitch appeared in their midst. He came riding in on a mule, the picture of a white *bwana* in boots, jodhpurs, and a pith helmet. At first the falashas hesitated, slow to give their hearts a second time.

"We have received no sign of sympathy from the white Jews," one of their leaders told Faitlovitch. "They know the road to come to us. We do not know the road to go to them. We have looked for the way. We want to go to Jerusalem, but we cannot find it. It is certain that not only is Joseph [Halévy] dead but also the other Jews of the whole world, and that they no longer exist on the earth, outside of here."

They were still suspicious, still wary of missionaries. "Every European who comes to us proclaims himself a Jew," they said, "but that is only to deceive us and convert us."

They insisted, by one account, that Faitlovitch make camp at the stream at the edge of their village. He had to spend seven

35

days in purification and prayer. Then they welcomed him into their house of prayer.

"Encompassed by the enemies of their religion, Ethiopia slept for near a thousand years," wrote historian Edward Gibbon, "forgetful of the world by whom they were forgotten." In this isolated land, no one felt more beset than the falashas. No one slept longer or dreamed deeper.

Now Jacques Faitlovitch stirred them awake. He was twenty-three years old, eager and generous, with a taste for adventure and the heart for a great cause. He brought the falashas the gift of hope and a promise that they would no longer be alone in the world. He learned their language, and he taught them their first words of Hebrew. At sunset, they talked endlessly, the Ethiopians and the European, catching each other up on two thousand years of history.

Faitlovitch lived among them for eighteen months on that first trip. Then, taking two young students with him, he returned to Europe to tell other Jews about them.

He returned to Ethiopia again and again. He was obsessed with educating and "normalizing" them. Sometimes they resisted the religious changes he was urging. Sometimes he hurt their feelings by rejecting their Ethiopian ways as "wrong." Yet word of him spread. As he approached one village, they came to meet him with singing, dancing, and prayer, as if he were a messiah.

Indeed, he was an earthly savior. He was their link to the outside world. If he did not stir a groundswell of interest in them, he did plant the seeds. In one country after another, in Europe and then in North America, he organized the first pro-falasha committees.

In Ethiopia, he set up the first falasha village school in 1913. A few years later, he returned with the two children he'd taken, grown men now, trained to be teachers of their people.

In 1920 he was searching for more bright youngsters. He hoped to create a chain of educated falashas who could pull their people up out of poverty and ignorance. He spent hours sitting under a tree in Wollaka, teaching Hebrew to a boy of eleven, Yonah Bogale. The boy's father was a weaver and tenant farmer, scratching out a living for eleven children. He was reluctant to send his son so far away, but he could see how eager the boy was.

Many years later, Yonah Bogale remembered his journey with Faitlovitch:

> We were a year on the way. First we traveled on foot and with mules. We came to Addis Ababa. There I saw electric lights and water faucets. There I saw automobiles driving in the street. I was amazed that a thing made of iron, with no horses to pull it, could run better than any animal, better than any man.
>
> Then we traveled to Jerusalem. My people have a great love for Jerusalem, but in our villages we couldn't dream what it would look like. I thought I would see a golden city, and it was very sad to look at how poor and dirty it was then, just like Addis.

Yonah studied in Jerusalem for three years, then spent nine more years in France, Italy, and Germany. He became learned in his religion, fluent in half a dozen languages, and at home in the great cities of Europe. When it was time to return to Ethiopia, he had mixed feelings. "I had to fight my own desires, but I had promised to go back."

"I had many things to say to our people about the Jews in other places," Yonah remembered. "I said that there are many white Jews in the world who are thinking of us. I said that they are not poor like us, but that many live in fine houses. I said that the Jewish people is a great people."

He had returned in 1932 to "a providence from God," a Jewish school that had been opened in Addis by Faitlovitch. The school was a collection of rented *tukuls* for classrooms and dormitories. Some of its eighty students were the children of falashas who'd been brought to Addis by force in the 1890s to work as masons and craftsmen on the emperor's new palaces and churches. For the chance to study, other students walked hundreds of miles from Gondar province to Addis. Some studied for two years and then were sent to universities abroad. Others returned to the falasha provinces as teachers at new village schools.

Unlike so much of Africa, Ethiopia had never been colonized and ruled by white foreigners. Then, in 1936, in a preamble to World War II, fascist Italy invaded and conquered Ethiopia. Haile Selassie pleaded in vain for help from the old League of Nations. "It is us today," he warned. "It will be you tomorrow."

Selassie took refuge in Jerusalem, where he was listed in the phone book, with full honors, as "Selassie, Haile *King.*" The school in Addis was closed, never to open again. Some of its teachers and students were arrested by the fascists, and Yonah became a fugitive. He hid among the Oromo tribesmen and worked as a supervisor in the gold mines. By legend, these are the gold fields of Queen Sheba, the "Ophir" mentioned in the Bible.

With the war, the falashas lost their lifeline to the outside world. Some of them joined the antifascist underground. Others fought and died as guerrilla soldiers for Ethiopia, but their patriotism went unrewarded. In 1946, when Faitlovitch visited them for the last time, he found their situation worse than ever.

Over the years Faitlovitch had arranged for forty students to study abroad. This first generation of educated falashas turned out to be remarkable. Some of them, restless now in their old villages, pursued government careers in Addis. They rose to high ranks. One became the minister of finance. Another was the ambassador to Rome. Yonah headed the Education Department for a while, until he quit to become the chief spokesman of his people.

In 1948 the most sophisticated bit of technology in the falasha villages was the portable radio. Over this, they heard that

Jews were fighting to establish a state of Israel. Some of the young men sent a letter to the Jewish Agency. "Help us to come to Jerusalem," they wrote, "so that we can fight by your side." Once again, there was no answer. The young nation was struggling to be born. She was battered by the wars with her Arab neighbors. There were desperate Jews in Europe and then in the Arab nations of Morocco, Yemen, and Iraq to bring home first.

Anxiously, the falashas waited for a *sheliach*, a messenger who would show them the road to Jerusalem. The young state of Israel had been created to gather in the exiles, and such messengers were dispatched to Jewish communities around the world. "Get ready," the falashas told themselves. "It will be our turn soon." But Israel was busy with other things. She did not know what to make of these strange people who called themselves Beta Israel. No messenger was sent to call them home.

Still, they were on the road to change. Faitlovitch, living in Israel now, struggled to arouse some interest in them. In 1954 he persuaded the Jewish Agency to open a new teacher-training school in Asmara. Over the next two years, American Mizrachi Women, a philanthropic society, brought twenty-seven falasha teenagers to live and study at Kfar Batya, a youth village in Israel. Faitlovitch was dying, but one of his last pleasures was a visit from a group of these students. In his will he left his house as a meeting place for these students and for other Ethiopian Jews who would come after them.

Progress came in fits and false starts. Two years after Faitlovitch's death, the school in Asmara was closed. When it was reopened in another village, Wuzaba, it was burned by angry Christians. "If we opened a school," Yonah remembered, "they thought we were trying to take over their land."

Then the first Kfar Batya teenagers returned to Ethiopia. As one of those students, now middle-aged, remembered recently, "We studied for three years. When we were about to leave Israel, President Ben Zvi and people from the Jewish Agency came to talk to us. 'Prepare your people for *aliyah,*'* they told us. When we arrived in our home, maybe a thousand people came to meet us, all of them ready to go to Jerusalem. 'We have come back to teach you,' we told them. 'Maybe next year you can go to Jerusalem.' "

The training school was reopened in Ambober, the largest all-falasha village, with Kfar Batya graduates as teachers. In twenty-seven scattered villages, small classrooms were set up to give little children what their parents had never had, the chance to learn to read and write. They were short-lived. After only a year or so, with the Jewish Agency claiming it had run out of funds, all the schools but the one in Ambober were closed.

Years later, some of them were reopened under the auspices of the Organization for Rehabilitation and Training (ORT), a nonprofit Jewish organization that also operates nonsectarian programs in many countries. Usually these village schools went only to the third grade. In Ambober, a village of three hundred *tukuls,* the school went only as far as sixth grade. Beyond that, there was an advanced Jewish school in Gondar city, the provincial capital. To educate their children, close-knit falasha families had to send them away to a distant town and somehow find the money for room and board. As one parent complained to his son, "I have to sell a cow for you every month."

Government schools were more accessible, but they made many falasha parents nervous. "Our children will forget our laws there. They will become unclean." For centuries they had kept their identity by keeping apart. Now, with each year, the temptations of the outside world grew. The missionaries saved lives at their medical clinics, but they dispensed religion there, too. They converted some falashas with a promise of better schooling and better jobs. Angrily, the Beta Israel accused them of "buying souls."

*The going-forth to Israel.

At the same time, there was a fever of Zionism in the falasha villages. In the old prayers they recited, the promise of a return to Jerusalem seemed more real, more imminent than ever before. "The people were ready. They were waiting to make *aliyah,*" the Kfar Batya graduate remembered. "When it didn't happen, they lost trust in us. We too despaired."

Without schools to teach in, few of them remained in the villages. After a few years, some returned to Israel to lobby the government. "Have we not suffered as Jews?" one of them asked. "Are we not still suffering?" Others found a different life, working in the industry and government of Ethiopia.

Yonah Bogale stayed among his people. Eloquent in several languages, with an impressive bearing, he became their liaison with the Jews of the world. When there was no more Jewish Agency money, funds came from the American Association for Ethiopian Jews and England's Falasha Welfare Organization.

Usually, Yonah had about thirty thousand dollars a year—a bit more than a dollar per falasha—to help his people survive. He tried to dole it out carefully. It is, for example, just a few hours' drive by Land Rover or rural bus from the provincial capital of Gondar to the village of Ambober. Yonah, aging now, made the trip in two days, walking the distance. He was saving money and he was not in a hurry. "I live on African time," he explained to an American visitor.

Wherever he went, Yonah was also a teacher. "The ideas and the customs of the other Jews of the world were strange to our people," he remembered. "It was hard for some to understand. They did not want to change the things that had kept us alive for generations, and there were some angry discussions."

Malka Alemie was a young mother, sitting apart with the other women, eavesdropping on Yonah's discussion with the men of her village. Faithfully, they had followed the Torah; now Yonah was telling them to accept the Talmud, too. Her grandfather, a *kes,* was skeptical. "Did God speak twice?" he asked.

"We read the Torah in the best way we could," Yonah tried to explain, "but maybe our interpretation was wrong. Maybe we made a mistake."

Malka did not speak, but she nodded as her grandfather answered, "And maybe it is they who made the mistake, not us."

The Beta Israel gave up some of their old practices, such as the animal sacrifices that dated back to the days of the Temple. They clung fast to other traditions, especially the menstrual hut, and layered on some new customs. Some of the men began to wear *kipas,* or skullcaps. The Star of David had been a more prominent symbol among Ethiopian Christians than Jews, but now they made it their own. It was forged and mounted on some houses of prayer, and many women embroidered it on their dresses.

Yonah stirred hope but also controversy. The Ethiopian Jews had no tradition of a single leader; each group of villages had its own leader, usually a *kes.* There was jealousy when foreign Jews treated Yonah as the chief of all 490 villages. The money from abroad arrived sporadically, less often and in smaller amounts than people thought, and some villages suspected they did not get their fair share. There were charges that Yonah spoke to visitors about Gondar province, where he lived, but somehow neglected to mention the falasha villages of Tigray province.

Still, Yonah was the spokesman his people needed, eloquent, persuasive, and persistent. Many Ethiopian Jews believe the *aliyah* would have taken even longer without him. In Israel, his sons have been embraced as a second generation of Beta Israel leaders.

In the second half of the twentieth century, the Ethiopian Jews swung between hope and disappointment. Again and again, the road to Jerusalem was blocked by the events of history and the ironies of geopolitics.

Israel had embarked on her African Policy. Surrounded by

Arab enemies, she was looking for friends beyond that hostile circle. Israel stretched out a hand to the developing countries of Africa, and no one grasped it more eagerly than Ethiopia. In the 1960s, Addis Ababa was crowded with Israeli advisers. They helped to train Ethiopia's army and organize her police force; they set up the nation's bus system and worked to improve her agriculture. With her strategic location on the Red Sea, Ethiopia was an important ally. With her historic ties to the ancient Israelites, she was a good friend to the modern ones.

Yet few of these Israeli visitors bothered to travel north to visit their falasha brethren, and the emperor's fondness for Israeli Jews did not extend to the home-grown variety. He would not revoke the old *falassi* edict and allow them to own land. Nor would he allow them to emigrate.

Selassie was trying to stitch together a modern nation out of the patchwork of minorities, warring tribes, and rebellious provinces that was Ethiopia. He worried that if one group tried to leave, if one thread were pulled, the whole fabric would unravel.

Behind his closed doors, though, Selassie sat on a shaky throne. In 1974 the old Lion of Judah was overthrown in a bloody revolution. Power was seized by a shadowy committee of 120 military men who called themselves the Dergue. Quickly, the new government became strongly Marxist. Four years and several shoot-outs later, there were only forty men left on the Dergue, and Lieutenant Colonel Mengistu Haile Mariam was their chairman.

The falashas had tried to stay neutral during the revolution, and at first they seemed to be its beneficiaries. In a program of land reform, the new rulers tore up the old *falassi* edict. For the first time in centuries, the Jews could own land. Yet they did not prosper. Often, the land they were given was worn out and rock-strewn. Often, the old landlords returned to burn the falasha houses and crops and chase the Jews off the land. Some of the Jews did hold on to their acres, but the old landlords were back at harvest time, demanding their traditional "rent"—a third to a half of the crops—and few falashas dared to refuse.

Like most Marxist governments, this one attacked religion. As bullies, they tiptoed around Ethiopia's two strongest religions—the Coptic majority and the powerful Moslem minority. Instead, they stepped hard on the smaller and weaker faiths—such Protestant groups as the Methodists, Pentecostals, and Seventh-Day Adventists, the Roman Catholics, and the Jews.

Followers of these "foreign religions," as they were labeled, were not allowed to celebrate their holidays openly, follow their special cultural and religious traditions, or worship freely. A number of the Protestant missions closed their doors, and their European leaders went home.

For the falashas, there had been small pockets of goodwill, created by the nonsectarian irrigation and road-building projects of ORT. Now the organization was expelled from Ethiopia. The ORT schools were closed and, for a time, so were the synagogues. Some Marxist officials developed a special excuse for hounding the falashas. As Jews, they were said to be pro-Israel, pro-American, and, in a wild leap, agents of the CIA.

Ethiopia had approved the Universal Declaration of Human Rights, and later the new government would sign the African Charter on Human and People's Rights, a document declaring that "everyone has the right to leave any country, including his own." Yet the new government locked its doors as tightly as the old one.

By now, after the Six-Day War of 1967 and the Yom Kippur War of 1973, Israel's Africa Policy was in ruins. Like most of the continent, Ethiopia had no diplomatic ties with the Jewish state. Addis was now crowded with a new group of "advisers," a growing army of Russians and Cubans who had a special reason—hostility to Israel—for locking the Jews in.

The new laws stirred old hatreds. The falashas were singled out by "the white terror," a reign of raids by the Ethiopian Democratic Union, a well-armed unit still loyal to Selassie.

Women were raped and mutilated, and men were castrated. There are reports that some falashas were captured and sold into slavery, an institution that refuses to die in Africa. The falashas were also a favorite target of "the red terror" that followed, raids by the Ethiopian People's Revolutionary Party, a Marxist group that opposed the Dergue.

Terror came in legal guise too, in the epauletted uniform of Major Malaka Tafara, the governor of Gondar province. Violently anti-Jewish, he blamed the Beta Israel for the famine and other Ethiopian catastrophes. Jews were humiliated and beaten. Hebrew, the rediscovered language of prayer, could no longer be taught. In some villages, the market day was changed to Saturday, to taunt the Jews into breaking their Sabbath. The Jews kept faith. "We will not sell our souls," they insisted. In other villages, though, they had to watch helplessly as holy books were burned and houses torched.

More than ever, the falashas felt like strangers in Ethiopia. Faitlovitch had told him they were no longer alone, and they had sent a message with him to the Jews of the world: "Peace! Peace! O, our brothers, do not forget us."

Now, at long last, there was an answer. Finally, the debate over the falashas, an argument that had lasted a hundred years, was settled. The Israelis agreed that they were indeed brothers.

The Sephardi Chief Rabbi of Israel, Ovadia Josef, had pored over the writings of the Radbaz and other sages. On February 9, 1973, he wrote his own opinion:

. . . the Falashas are descended from the tribes of Israel who traveled southward to Ethiopia. There is no doubt that . . . they are of the tribe of Dan. . . . I have decided, in my humble opinion, that they are Jews who must be saved from absorption and assimilation. We are obligated to speed up their immigration into Israel and to educate them in our Holy Torah, making them partners in the building up of our land. *And the sons shall return to the Holy Land.*

I am certain that government institutions and the Jewish Agency, as well as organizations in Israel and in the Diaspora, will help us to the best of their ability in this holy task . . . the mitzvah [good deed] of redeeming the souls of our people. *For whoever saves a single soul . . . it is as though he had saved a whole world.*

Two years later, the Ashkenazi Chief Rabbi, Shlomo Goren, agreed. In 1975, the government of Israel said its own amen, decreeing that the Beta Israel were like any other Jews, eligible under the Law of Return. Like any other Jews, they could come to Israel and be her citizens.

Yet though Israel was now willing to let them in, Ethiopia was still unwilling to let them out. With the help of the Jewish Agency, some of Yonah Bogale's children had managed to leave, as "students." In 1979, with the help of the American Association for Ethiopian Jews, the door was opened just wide enough for Yonah and his wife to slip through.

Under the Ethiopian system, they had to leave a guarantee behind, two hostages: Yonah's brother and one of his daughters. If someone did not return, the hostages would be put in prison and their homes and property seized. Yonah stayed in Israel, where his voice was still needed. His wife was able to see the promised land, but then, to save the hostages, she had to return to Ethiopia.

In that same year, 1979, letters were sent to Ethiopia, and at last a *sheliach* was dispatched to the falashas. A Kfar Batya student returned, carrying a message of hope and danger. As he told them, the road to Israel was open, but it led over the mountains, across the desert, and into Sudan.

# Chapter 6

# "The Lone Rangers"

*"I KNOW THEY ARE hiding somewhere,"* the army captain insisted. Even in the blazing summer heat of Sudan, even in the dust of a front yard in the sprawling, unpaved city of Gedaref, the captain looked dapper in his uniform.

He was speaking to the young Ethiopian who did gardening and other odd jobs for him. He was fond of this tall and bony fellow, so street-wise behind the sweet, lopsided smile.

"Listen, Hassan," the captain said. "If you help me to find those black Jews, I'll pay you."

"Black Jews, my captain?" The young man looked puzzled. "What do you mean? I thought Jews were white."

The young man admired the captain, but he lied for a living. He was not "Hassan," and not the Moslem he pretended to be. He was Gideon, a black Jew himself, one of the secret messengers.

In 1980, searching out a route that others would then follow, he was one of the first to make the trek to Sudan. Crossing the border, Gideon had been stopped and questioned by the captain.

"I am Hassan, a poor Moslem," Gideon began, offering a humble smile. "I am looking for work. There is none in Ethiopia for Moslems."

The captain's aide reached for the small bundle that Gideon carried. He pulled out an extra shirt. Then a water flask. Then Gideon's only possession of value, the transcript of his school records, with his real name and Jewish identity.

The captain reached for the folded paper. "Really?" he was asking. "Are you a good worker?" Gideon nodded, swallowing, unable to speak.

The captain was unfolding the paper. Then, preoccupied, he stopped. Something else had occurred to him. He smiled at Gideon. "Do you know about gardening?" Explaining how to find his house, the captain returned the paper, still unread, to Gideon.

Months later, in the garden, the captain's guess was right. By now, there were two thousand Ethiopian Jews in Sudan, some trying to hide in the *tukuls* of Gedaref, others keeping low in the refugee camps that were growing like weeds in the countryside. Gideon was personally responsible for some of the Jews being there.

"My mother is crying in Ethiopia," the young man lied one day. "She wants to see my face." He gave the captain a helpless shrug. "You know how mothers are."

The captain smiled. "Here," he said, signing a travel pass to the border for Gideon.

In truth, Gideon's mother was hiding in a small *tukul* in Gedaref, paid for by her son's wages as the captain's gardener. Gideon wanted to slip back into Ethiopia for another reason—to help lead a group of eighty-five Jews along the secret roads to Sudan.

"I am young and strong," Gideon told his mother. "If I don't help our people, who will?" He made that dangerous trip on his own, but now he met others who wanted to help.

"Listen, Gideon," an Ethiopian friend told him one day. "There's a Jew from America in town. He's looking for someone like you, someone who speaks English and Amharic."

In the gloom of his friend's *tukul,* Gideon met the white man, a member of the American Association for Ethiopian Jews (AAEJ), an activist group, zealous and impatient. Gideon had heard about them. In American and Israeli cities, they championed the cause of the Beta Israel. They pressed the members of Congress in Washington and the Knesset in Jerusalem. In Ethiopia and then Sudan, they smuggled in money and hope—and sometimes smuggled out people.

"We need information," the man explained. "So we can help your people. So we can tell the world about them."

At a time when few people had ever heard of the falashas, Gideon understood that AAEJ was stirring support for them. Other groups—including the militant Canadian Association for Ethiopian Jews and the calmer, more cooperative North American Conference on Ethiopian Jewry—also tried to help. Long before the main-line Jewish organizations took up the cause, these people led it. In years when Israel and America both were struggling with so many other crises, they would not allow the lost Jews to be forgotten once again.

With his loose-limbed, loping walk and crooked grin, Gideon prowled the unpaved streets of Gedaref for the AAEJ and roamed the camps. He became a messenger, a translator, and a gatherer of the information that they needed—who are the Jews, where are they, what can we do to help?

One of AAEJ's leaders was a wealthy New York businessman, edgy, stoop-shouldered, middle-aged. He'd lost his parents in the Holocaust, and he would not let other Jews be trapped again. Harmless looking in his ill-fitting suits, he was the last man Sudanese officials would suspect of setting up escape routes and spiriting people out. He recruited an unlikely

A-Team—Ethiopians like Gideon, a few adventurous Americans in blue jeans, and some Orthodox Jews. One of them had to be reminded to take off his Star of David and check his phylacteries at the airport before going ahead with his secret mission.

After a while, an AAEJ agent found a way to slip Gideon's mother out of Sudan and into Israel. Gideon could have gone, too, but he stayed behind. He was a pipeline between his people, clinging together, fearful and suspicious, and the impassioned, impatient strangers who wanted to help.

In Gedaref, though, the Sudanese captain never lost his own passion for ferreting out the hidden Jews. "I have figured out how to do it," he told Gideon one afternoon. "Those Jews don't light fires on their Sabbath. So on Friday night, we shall see which houses are dark."

"Ah, my captain," Gideon agreed, "that's very clever."

That night, he hurried along the narrow streets and alleyways, a scrawny, dark-skinned Paul Revere, spreading a warning from house to house. "Listen," he told the hidden Jews, "you must light a fire this Friday night." Even on the dangerous trek from Ethiopia, these people had stopped to keep the Sabbath; now Gideon told them they must break it. "To save a life, it is permitted," he insisted. "Don't use it. Don't cook on it. But you must have it."

In truth, they were enemies, this Moslem army officer and this young believer in the Zionist dream. In the lies that Gideon told, they grew to like each other. "In Ethiopia, Moslems are poor," Gideon had told the captain, to explain why he knew only a few words of Arabic. "We don't have our own schools." Using English, a language they'd both learned at government schools, they often talked together.

Each week, Gideon shook his head when the captain invited him to pray at the nearby mosque. One Friday, the Moslem Sabbath, the captain announced, "No more excuses. Today you're going." With a firm grip on Gideon's arm, he pulled him along to the mosque.

In the cool interior, Gideon moved his lips silently, pretending to pray. He watched the captain carefully, trying to stand or kneel on the prayer rug at the right times. Two or three times, though, Gideon was still bent down bowing when everyone else was up.

As they walked home, the captain's mouth was a tight, angry line. "You pray like no Moslem I ever saw," he muttered.

Gideon shrugged helplessly, struggling to keep the fear out of his voice. "It's different in Ethiopia," he tried to explain. "And my family is not religious."

That afternoon, he dug busily in the garden. When he looked up, he caught the captain's stare, suspicious and still angry.

The next day, Saturday, Gideon stayed away. He never worked on Saturdays. Another lie. He'd told the captain he met with a study group that day, to improve his English. Instead, on the Sabbath, he met with other hidden Jews in a clandestine prayer service.

Nervously, Gideon returned to the captain's house a few days later. There were travel passes to be gotten from the officer, and sometimes he dropped bits of information that were helpful to the Beta Israel. Yet Gideon knew that if the captain guessed he was a Jew, he would be bound for jail.

That week, the captain was cool to him, and Gideon felt himself being watched. That Friday, the captain didn't invite him to the mosque, but he pushed a book at him, a new English translation of the Koran. "Here, I bought this for you," he said gruffly. "Study it."

Gideon did study it. Some of it sounded to him like the wisdom of the Torah. He was carrying it the day he led a white man, a relief worker, from Gedaref to the Um Rakuba camp. Along sixty miles of rutted road, on a bus that wheezed with age, it was a punishing three-hour ride.

Um Rakuba was a monument to nature's cruelty—and man's. The camp had been built for the refugees of the 1974 drought, and it grew, acre by grim acre, with the endless droughts and civil wars that followed. Now it was a city of despair, its straw *tukuls* crowded close together, a dozen or more people huddled in each.

It was a place for people with no place to go. Disease flourished here—malaria, dysentery, and fevers; though no official wanted to name them, there are reports of typhus and cholera. People died here. So did hope.

For Gideon's people, there were special terrors. As Jews, they were frightened at being in a Moslem land. As falashas, they were often tormented by their old neighbors, the other refugees from Ethiopia. "Some families are too sick and too afraid to leave the *tukul,*" Gideon told the man. "Only once a day, one person goes out for the food."

Gideon and the white man moved along the narrow, muddy pathways. In the swelter of the Sudan summer night, in the miasma of disease and decay, in the stench of so many wretched bodies, the sweating man paused. Like most Westerners, he carried a bottle of water everywhere. Gulping some of it down, he sighed, "That's the twelfth bottle today."

Finally, they reached the *tukul* where a group of Jews waited. "I am here to help," the man began, and Gideon translated from his English to their Amharic. Yet there was a gaping sore here, and the relief worker had little more than sympathy to offer.

"We are doing all we can," the Israeli government had insisted. Secrecy was vital, and the government was disarmed, unable to answer its critics. To prove that more could be done, AAEJ had begun to stage its own rescue operations.

They started in early 1980, by acquiring twenty-four false passports. Loaded in a truck, heads down at the army checkpoints, the refugees were smuggled from Gedaref to Khartoum, more than two hundred miles away. There they were handed the forged documents and put on a plane to West Germany.*

Now Gideon's work became more dangerous. One night, toward the end of April 1983, he gathered a group of Jews who had been hiding in the Gedaref *tukuls.* The plan was to lead them along a new escape route out of Sudan; if they made it, others would follow.

"Quickly," he whispered. "Quietly." He shepherded them through the dusty alleyways. Each time he looked back, the parade of people following him seemed to have grown larger. By the time they reached a dry riverbed at the edge of town, there were fifty falashas.

A white Toyota van was parked in the night shadows. Next to it waited a burly, red-bearded American. Gideon grinned with admiration at the man's cowboy hat, but the face under the big brim was angry.

"What's going on?" the American demanded. "Who are all these people?" An AAEJ volunteer, just arrived in Sudan, he had expected to drive a dozen or so people to freedom. Instead, he growled, "It looks like we're holding a market day."

"Okay, it's okay," Gideon said, proud of his American slang. "They are here to say good-bye."

The American, whom we'll call "Red," stared at the excited crowd. "There's only one van," he worried. "There'll be a riot when they all try to push into it."

"No, no," Gideon insisted, serious now. "Our people are not like that. Our people do not push." He moved from one knot of people to another. There were final embraces, whispered last words, and then the crowd dwindled, friends and relatives fading back into the shadows of Gedaref.

---

*Later it would turn out that not all the black refugees were Jews. In the past, to save their lives, Jews had sometimes disguised themselves as Christians. Now, perhaps for the first time in history, Christians were pretending to be Jews. Thus, fourteen of the refugees would remain in Germany; the rest would be taken to Israel.

Eighteen men, women, and children remained, and Gideon crammed them into the van. It was a tight squeeze, and Gideon gave Red a helpless smile. "The children are small," he explained. "The people are skinny."

Counting Gideon, Red, and a third man, an Ethiopian Christian who had resettled in Sudan and knew the route, there were twenty-one people in the little van. The youngest passenger was two months old; the oldest was a man of seventy-three.

With a shrug, Red started the engine. He felt happy to be back in Africa, his first trip since he'd been a young Peace Corps worker in Nigeria. Married now, with two young children, he'd taken a month's leave from his corporate job on America's West Coast. He had followed a zigzag route. First stop was Nairobi, the capital of Kenya, for a briefing at the apartment AAEJ kept for agents like him. Then a quick flight to Juba, the southern capital of Sudan, and a plane to Khartoum.

He spent two weeks in Khartoum, getting his Africa legs back, relearning Africa's mysteries. Yet as he drove from Khartoum to Gedaref, he knew he'd broken the cardinal rule for traveling through her deserts and backlands. He needed a sturdier vehicle, with four-wheel drive, but the Toyota van was all he'd been able to rent. He'd stocked it with blankets, malaria pills, and water bottles for the passengers.

"Watch out for the gas," he instructed now. Getting fuel had been his biggest problem so far. He had spent days getting permits in Khartoum and then searching for stations that had some gas for sale.

"No smoking," he warned Gideon, who had picked up the habit from his Sudanese captain. Red had crammed sixteen plastic jugs into the back of the van. Once they had held peanut oil; now each contained five gallons of gas. He had bought the last five gallons on the black market in Gedaref, "just for practice." It was enough gas for the trip he was planning, but not for the one he would eventually make.

They drove west, moving fast, pushing the overloaded van at

seventy-five miles per hour. Then Gideon tensed, spotting the first checkpoint. If the guards asked for papers, Red was the only one in the van with a legal pass to travel this road. "I work for Chevron," he had lied, dropping the name of the American oil company that was planning a pipeline in Sudan. "I want to travel around," he had told the officials in Khartoum, "and see your beautiful country."

At the checkpoint, Red kept a heavy foot on the gas pedal. Leaning out the window, he grinned at the guard and waved his cowboy hat. Without stopping, he drove through.

"I'm invisible," he explained, winking at Gideon. He was counting on a hangover from colonial days, the cautious respect for white men that was still common in Africa. "I'm harmless, just a friendly white man. It's illegal Africans they're checking for."

With a wave of Red's hat, they raced past the next couple of checkpoints. Under the stars near the desert village of Jebble Fool, they could make out the silhouette of a tent and the shadowed humps of a camel caravan bedded down for the night. "I saw them earlier today, when I checked the road," Red said. "A hundred camels. Imagine. That's got to be worth a fortune."

At the bridge at Wad Medani, the road forked north to Khartoum and south to Juba. Here, two trucks were stopped ahead of them at the checkpoint, and they too had to stop.

"How ya doing?" Red grinned at the guard, when it was their turn. He handed over his pass, but the guard was not satisfied. He peered into the van.

"Who are these other people?" he wanted to know. "Where are their papers?"

"Here they are." Red smiled, but his hands were clammy as he handed over a wad of one hundred Sudanese pounds (about sixty American dollars). Sometimes baksheesh can be a passport, but not always. This time, the guard counted the bills, then waved the van through.

Now they turned south, moving fast, churning up a hot breeze. At three in the morning, eight hours after leaving Gedaref, they drove into the sleeping village of Rabak and parked next to a straw hut, a "safe house" belonging to a family of Ethiopian Christians.

The passengers clambered out, tired but jubilant. Gideon grinned. "They think they are already saved." They had been plucked from their refugee huts. A white Jew from faraway America had brought them clean blankets and good water. He was driving them to freedom in a van—crowded, but first-class travel for people used to walking. Surely Jerusalem could not be far away.

Red sighed. Jerusalem was in the other direction, to the north, but safety lay in this long way around. This was as far as he planned to go, but the hard part was still ahead for his passengers.

When they had rested, the woman of the house used a pounding stick to grind the beans for glasses of strong black coffee, lifeblood for Ethiopians, Christians and Jews alike.

As they drank, Gideon told the American about his passengers. "The old man," he said, "is a great one." His name was Mengistu Elias. In 1920, he'd been one of the young boys taken out of the falasha villages by Jacques Faitlovitch, to be educated in Europe. He'd returned as a teacher and leader of his people. Now he was seventy-three, tall and white-haired. If AAEJ could bring this well-known falasha to Jerusalem, it would help to call attention to his people's cause.

Over uncounted glasses of coffee, Red explained the plan to his passengers. He and Gideon would return to Gedaref for a second load of refugees. The others were to go to the truck station and buy passage on a truck going south to Juba. Smiling, the falashas nodded. In the African backlands, trucks often served as the rural "bus system." Wide-eyed, they took the envelopes Red had prepared, 150 Sudanese pounds for everyone old enough to walk. It was more money than they'd ever seen at one time. Red explained that they would have to pay 90 pounds of it each for the truck ride.

Carefully, they passed along the directions, from Red to Gideon to the others, from English to Amharic and then, to be sure they understood, back again. Over and over, back and forth, like a life-and-death game of "Telephone," they repeated the details. The safe address in Juba. The rendezvous—a market by day, a restaurant by night—where they would meet the contact who would take them farther along. The code names to use. The places to hide if things went wrong.

Aside from Mengistu, these were simple villagers, traveling a dangerous road without papers. Did they understand? Would they remember? It was an untested escape route, and Gideon was worried. He could smile and lie his way through; Red could bluff and bully the guards along the way. Without them, could the people make it?

Uneasy, with a farewell wave of Red's cowboy hat, they drove off. At the edge of town, they felt the van swerve to the left and heard the flopping sound of a tire gone flat. They limped to a "garage," a straw lean-to propped up in a yard littered with the bits and pieces, the "spare parts," of wrecked vehicles. Red paced up and down as the mechanic patched the tire.

"Maybe we're not supposed to leave these people," he told Gideon. "Maybe the flat tire is a sign."

"Yes, yes," Gideon agreed. "A sign." He was grinning as they returned to the safe house.

White-haired Mengistu met them. "May the Lord make his face to shine upon you," he blessed Red, offering a gift, an ancient tallith, or prayer shawl.

"A little farther," Red promised. "I'll take you a little farther." Maybe he could buy papers for them at the next town, before putting them on the trucks.

Red tried to get some rest, but he had barely dozed off when Gideon was shaking him. "These people are asking too many questions," he said. "Maybe this safe house isn't so safe." Red nodded. It was early afternoon, but safer to go than to stay.

The paved road ended at Rabak. Now they were bouncing along a dirt road, a washboard of ruts that was the main north-south "highway" of Sudan. They were moving through a bleak and barren landscape, but Gideon pointed suddenly. "Look!" His people had come from the land where the Blue Nile begins. Now they were following the course of another river. There, glinting in the sun, was the White Nile.

A few miles later, the van faltered, sputtered, and stopped dead. Red was checking under the hood, trying to figure out what was wrong, when a truck lumbered to a stop behind them. Quickly, the driver found the problem. "The distributor," he announced.

Red groaned. In the middle of the desert, where was he going to find new distributor points? "New?" the driver asked. "You don't need new." From the cab of his truck he produced sheets of sandpaper. Then he showed them how to smooth down the distributor points. "Good as new," he told them.

With a wave of Red's cowboy hat, they were off again. In the Peace Corps, he'd learned to drive these washboard roads. "We can go very slow, five or six miles an hour," he told Gideon, "or very fast, fifty or sixty miles an hour." He stepped heavily on the gas pedal, choosing speed. His passengers sat quiet, patient, uncomplaining, as Red squinted ahead. In the headlights' beam, it was hard to tell where the road ended and the desert began. The trick was to find your own piece of road, between the ruts other vehicles had made, and still stay on the road.

Hour after hour they drove, other headlights passing now and then. They had left Rabak at two in the afternoon, the sun beating down, turning the van into an oven on wheels. With darkness, it was cooler, though still steamy. Finally, at two in the morning, they bounced into the town of Renk. Here, amid a cluster of displaced Ethiopian Christians, there was another safe house, a straw hut where the people could rest.

In the morning, there was another flat tire to be fixed. At an open-air market, Red hunted down a few gallons of black-market gas, some tire irons, and sandpaper, "for the next emergency." At the compound of government and military offices, he shopped for papers for his passengers.

"We're going south," he told the town officials, "and I have these people with me. Can't we get some passes for them?"

"Where do these people come from?" the officials asked. "Why are they going south? Are they spies?"

Red pretended not to understand the questions. His offer to pay for the passes was refused. "These people are not legal," the officials decided. "You must take them back to Gedaref." As he left, the official shouted after him, "Do you understand? Back to Gedaref."

Red understood. It was an official order. If he wasn't planning to obey, it wasn't safe to linger here. Checking to be sure he wasn't followed, he drove back to the safe house.

Gideon was waiting for him, with white-haired Mengistu. Red had worried about the man's age, but so far he hadn't wilted. Quietly, he'd made himself leader, peacekeeper, spokesman for the passengers in the back of the van. "He's the strongest one of us," Red thought.

"Do you know what this is?" Mengistu asked, his eyes dark and unwavering. "This is the Passover."

Red nodded. A month earlier, Red in his comfortable suburban home, Gideon and Mengistu in their refugee huts, had celebrated the Jewish holiday of Passover, retelling the story of the first exodus out of Egypt. A world apart, they had said the same words: "Next year in Jerusalem."

The old man meant the reality of Passover, not the holiday. They were reliving the story, making the escape out of bondage, traveling through the desert, following a long, roundabout road to the promised land. Gideon and the old man were asking him not to abandon the people.

Red smiled, his mind made up. "Okay," he told them. "This year in Jerusalem. I'll take you as far as I can."

They left at six that evening. In the gathering twilight, they could see the desert, barren and endless. There were checkpoints at every town and bridge but, with nightfall, most of them were unmanned. Red grinned. "The soldiers are home sleeping."

Toward midnight, the van sputtered again. "Damn," Red swore. "The distributor again." He climbed out, ready to sand down the distributor points.

A passing truck braked to a stop next to them, and half a dozen Sudanese soldiers climbed out of the back. "If they ask for papers," Gideon whispered, "we are finished."

Suddenly, he was grinning again. The soldiers had stopped to help the stranded van. "Tell them we're okay," Red instructed. "Tell them to drive on."

Nodding, smiling, the driver and two of the soldiers peered over Red's shoulder. Then they opened the hood of the truck. They had a problem of their own, and so long as they had stopped, they would fix it here.

Nervously, Red looked around. Half his passengers had disappeared. "Where the hell are the women?" he hissed at Gideon.

"In the bushes." Gideon pointed to the scrub growth at the side of the road. The women were hiding there, terrified that the soldiers would rape and then murder them. Red nodded grimly. In Sudan, anything could happen to his black passengers, no questions asked. They lacked his special armor, a white skin. "They'll never bother an American," he'd boasted to Gideon. Yet he knew that wasn't completely true, and he had taken the time to arrange his affairs and write his will before leaving home.

He would have to stall. The women wouldn't return until the

soldiers were gone. He worked slowly, sanding the distributor points. One of the soldiers was making idle conversation with Gideon.

"Where are you headed?"

"North," Gideon lied, out of habit. Red saw him pointing and groaned. Now, even if the women hadn't disappeared, he didn't dare budge until the soldiers were well out of sight. He fussed with the van, cleaning the windshield, checking the tires, outwaiting them.

At last, the truck's hood was slammed shut. When its lights had disappeared, Gideon moved through the scrub bushes, calling softly, gathering up the women. When they had loaded the van, he realized someone was still missing. Gideon searched for the woman, the thorny bushes scratching his bare arms. It was ten minutes before he could find her, still crouched in terror.

Hour after hour, at sixty miles per hour, they bounced along. The back door of the van was rattling, banging open and shut, its latches jarred loose. There was an odd thud, and then another one. "Stop!" Gideon shouted. "Stop!" The plastic jugs of gas were tumbling out of the open rear door. He raced back down the road to retrieve the precious cargo.

They made rest stops when the van, faltering under the rough ride, forced them to. That night, they stopped three more times, twice to pick up falling jugs of gas, once to fix the distributor.

Finally, at nine the next morning, they reached the bridge at Malaka and drove past the deserted checkpoint. Its guard, late for work, was pedaling toward them on a bicycle. "Halt!" he shouted at them, waving at the checkpoint. "Halt!"

Red kept going, picking up speed. The soldier turned his bike around, shouting and pedaling furiously after the van, but they were moving too fast for him.

With no address for a safe house in Malaka, Red drove past the town, stopping finally at a "suburb," a cluster of straw huts. Here, Gideon paid the villagers a few pounds and asked them to provide drinking water and a hut where the people could rest. One of the villagers invited Red to his house to use a rare contraption, a bucket shower. For the first time since leaving Gedaref, he was able to get cleaned up.

Then Red and Gideon drove back to the town. They found a blacksmith who could weld the van's broken door. Then they located the town's Ministry of Supply. "I'm with Chevron," Red lied once again. This time, the official was friendly. To help the American "tourist" get to Juba, he signed a chit for twenty gallons of gas.

They strolled through the town, a few low concrete-block buildings and a sprawl of *tukuls.* "Let's find the Howard Johnson's," Red suggested. It was his name for Sudan's roadside stands, straw huts where truck drivers and other travelers could buy warm drinks and some food. At the Malaka food stand, they bought the local flatbread. "Like *injera,*" Gideon commented. Then they brushed the flies from a display of roast chickens, and bought them all, a feast for all the passengers.

At sunset, the van sagging under its heavy load, they were moving again. At a pontoon bridge leading across the wide, lazy White Nile and out of Malaka, they stopped at the checkpoint.

"Where are you going?" the guard asked in English.

Red smiled. "Juba."

"And these other people?"

"Juba."

The guard's mouth was open, framing another question, but Red's foot was pressing on the gas, pushing the van across the bridge. At Malaka they left the desert behind and entered a swampy territory. For a time, a gazelle, swift and graceful, raced alongside the van, keeping pace with it, then dropping back into the shadows.

Dawn was coming up when they stopped, fifty miles from Juba. They had moved out of the swamp and into a gentle, green countryside. They spotted monkeys swinging through the trees. Then Gideon grinned and the falasha women giggled and pointed. Moving toward them, leading a herd of

View of a typical village of *tukuls* in the Semien Mountains. Taken around 1907 by one of the first white Jews to reach the falasha villages. *(From Felix Rosen,* Eine deutsche Gesandtschaft in Abessinien [*A German Journey in Ethiopia*]. *Leipzig: Verlag Von Veit, 1907.)*

Two youngsters surrounded by the pottery that their mothers have produced. Beta Israel women made large and small vessels for daily use and also fashioned decorative figurines. Such crafts were despised in Ethiopia as the work of *buda,* or witches. *(From* Eine deutsche Gesandtschaft in Abessinien.)*

Ethiopian Jews at the turn of the century. These men are wrapped in the *shammas* that were still worn at the time of Operation Moses, and they carry the walking sticks that helped the falashas on their exodus. *(From Eine deutsche Gesandtschaft in Abessinien.)*

A village synagogue in Gondar province, unchanging from 1907 to the 1980s. *(From Eine deutsche Gesandtschaft in Abessinien.)*

Henry Stern preaching to the falashas at Sharger. A German Jew who was converted to Christianity in London, Stern became a missionary and was sent to Ethiopia in 1860. *(Engraving by J. Johnston. From Henry Stern,* Wandering Among the Falashas in Abyssinia. *London, 1862.)*

Jacques Faitlovitch *(center)* with Gete Jeremias *(right)* and Taamrat Emanuel in Florence about 1906. Faitlovitch brought these first falasha students to Europe to be educated and to tell the world about their tribe. *(Courtesy of the Faitlovitch Collection of the Elias Sourasky Central Library, Tel Aviv University.)*

Jacques Faitlovitch, the French Jew who became the savior of the falashas, with some of the young boys whom he took out of Ethiopia to be educated in Jerusalem, where this picture was taken, and the capitals of Europe. Among this group, in 1921, was Yonah Bogale *(second from left),* who would become the leader and teacher of his people, preparing them for the exodus. *(Courtesy of the Graenum Berger Collection.)*

Yonah Bogale today, the patriarch of his people, in front of his home in Israel. *(Photo by John Milton Williams.)*

Hebrew lesson at the Addis Ababa school started by Faitlovitch, 1924. *(Courtesy of the Faitlovitch Collection of the Elias Sourasky Central Library, Tel Aviv University.)*

Marketplace in Addis Ababa, c. 1924. *(Courtesy of the Faitlovitch Collection of the Elias Sourasky Central Library, Tel Aviv University.)*

Beta Israel soldier who fought in the Ethiopian Army during the Italian invasion, 1935. *(Courtesy of the Faitlovitch Collection of the Elias Sourasky Central Library, Tel Aviv University.)*

Another view of a falasha village, this one in the province of Gondar. *(Courtesy of the Graenum Berger Collection.)*

A Beta Israelite, a tenant farmer, plows his stony field. Even in "good times," before the 1984 famine, the oxen were poor and scrawny beasts. *(Courtesy of the Graenum Berger Collection.)*

Winnowing the Ethiopian grain *(tef)* in Wolleka, Ethiopia, 1984. *(Photo by Doron Bacher. Courtesy of Beth Hatefutsoth, The Nahum Goldmann Museum of the Jewish Diaspora.)*

Woman grinding *tef* on a grind-stone outside a hut in Wolleka. *(Photo by Doron Bacher. Courtesy of Beth Hatefutsoth, The Nahum Goldmann Museum of the Jewish Diaspora.)*

Carrying their ceremonial umbrellas, white-turbaned priests lead a funeral procession. *(Courtesy of the Graenum Berger Collection.)*

cows, was a small group of tribal Nubians, dark as night, naked as truth.

They had left Gedaref five days and eight hundred miles ago. Gideon leaned out the window, savoring the light rain that fell as they drove through the streets of Juba. Here, they delivered the dazed passengers to another safe house, a straw hut in a quiet grove of trees.

"And now?" Gideon asked. Red drove to the small Juba airport, hanging about until he saw a familiar face, a pilot who made regular runs between Juba and Nairobi. They had met at the AAEJ apartment in Nairobi, and the pilot agreed to take a message there: "We made it!"

The next day, Red and Gideon took two of the men through the back lanes of Juba to the crowded market where they were to wait each day, pretending to shop, for the next contact. While Red rehearsed the code names with them, Gideon poked among the open stalls where they sold secondhand clothing from America. There were no cowboy hats, "like Red's," but he settled happily on a jaunty fedora.

A few days later, the contact arrived, with a sturdy Land Rover to take the passengers across the border and on to Nairobi. Here, up the first flights of stairs they had ever climbed, was a different kind of safe house—an apartment. A birdlike American woman clucked over them and brought them food and new clothes. An Israeli representative made the final arrangements for them to board an El Al jetliner that landed in Nairobi once or twice a week and then flew directly to Israel.

Sometimes, other passengers had to be "bumped" to make room for the falashas. On this first trip, a man and wife from South Africa complained about being seated next to a black child. An Indian passenger offered to change seats with the child, but the couple objected to sitting next to him, too. Finally, the flight attendant told the South Africans, "If your seats aren't satisfactory, you can leave the plane."

Meanwhile, Gideon and Red were headed for the Juba airport. "No way we're going to drive back," Red announced. Already he was late getting back to his corporate job, and the van would never survive a return trip. Later, he would write to the rental company about where to retrieve their vehicle; they'd write back, with an invoice for freight charges and two extra months' rental, for a total bill of 8,490 Sudanese pounds ($4,540).

At the airport, Gideon wore his new fedora and a worried look. "I have no papers," he reminded the American.

"Don't worry," Red insisted. "I'll tell them you're my houseboy."

No one seemed to care. No questions were asked. If you could afford the ticket, you could board the plane. On the flight to Khartoum, Red and Gideon grinned at each other in triumph. They'd pioneered a new land escape and now, serendipitously, they'd discovered a second route, by air.

In Khartoum, Red dispensed a bit of baksheesh for the travel pass Gideon needed, then put his young friend on a truck bound for Gedaref. Gideon sighed happily as he bumped along. Soon the AAEJ would send money for the plane fares. Soon other falashas would be flying to freedom.

In government offices in Jerusalem and Washington, they called groups like AAEJ "the crazies" or, in kinder moments, "the Lone Rangers." They saw themselves as gadflies; whenever they felt Israel wasn't doing enough, they would prod her into action.

They were passionate men, risking their lives in Africa, pressing hard in Israel and the United States. In July 1983, they were a major force behind the passage of a Sense of the Congress resolution. It urged President Reagan to: "(1) express to relevant foreign governments the United States' concern for the welfare of the Ethiopian Jews, in particular their right to emigrate; (2) seek ways to assist Ethiopian Jews through every available means so that they may be able to emigrate freely."

At other times, their rhetoric was overheated. In print and on public platforms, they accused Israel of standing idly by while "a black holocaust" took place. The Israelis were furious; they did not need the AAEJ to teach them about holocausts. As Moshe Gilboa, of the Foreign Ministry in Israel, said angrily, "You don't have to smear three and a half million Jews in Israel in order to love twenty-eight thousand in Ethiopia."

The Israeli government was doing more, much more, than the AAEJ knew about. And the Israelis fervently wished that the American group would do less. The AAEJ were amateurs who sometimes, unwittingly, tripped up an operation that the professionals were planning. The Mossad complained that, in their zeal, they exposed some routes that could still have been used.

Gideon followed the road to Juba three times, but he was lucky enough to miss the operation on which two of AAEJ's agents were arrested there. Their small aircraft, a safari charter, was carrying passengers, six falashas. When they were apprehended, the two agents—an Irish-American and an American Jew—claimed they were chaperoning their passengers to colleges in other countries. Yet they had no travel documents, even forged ones, for them, and their "college student" passengers were illiterate, like most Ethiopians.

The Americans were charged with "slave trade" and taken to jail. At the news, Senator Charles Percy of Illinois expressed his concern to the Sudan embassy in Washington. The Americans were released, rearrested, and then released again after the U.S. embassy in Khartoum offered to hire a private plane to fly them out. As the Sudanese would admit later, they didn't want an incident to mar the coming visit of their president to Washington.

More than once, the AAEJ bumbled. More than once, governments were annoyed and embarrassed. Yet it had an unexpected result.

When American officials met with Sudanese leaders, to discuss an agenda of mutual concerns, they talked about these amateur rescue attempts. For its part, Sudan yearned to be rid of "the Lone Rangers." They became one of the urgent arguments in favor of letting the Jews go.

# Chapter 7

# The Mossad Connection

LONG BEFORE OPERATION Moses, there was another secret operation. Or a series of them.

These were Israeli operations, and among the best-kept secrets of our century. They started, and they stopped. Now and then, because of a slip, new plans had to be made and new routes found.

For seven long years, the operations were nameless, clandestine, unheralded. Somehow, more than six thousand falashas arrived in Israel. "Not by osmosis," said Yehuda Dominitz, the Jewish Agency's sly fox. Somehow, the black faces went unremarked in this small, mostly white country. They were dispersed, often out of sight in absorption centers.

Even the people who were rescued were in the dark, unaware of what was happening or how. They were falashas no more; they were Israelis now. At times they emerged from the shadows, clamoring for attention. In public demonstrations, they complained that not enough was being done for the people still trapped in Africa.

At times they were right, and the rescues were going too

67

slowly. At other times, even as they demonstrated, operations were under way. But these quiet people were tired of silence, weary of waiting, impatient with warnings that publicity could cost lives. "If we keep quiet," said Zachariah Yonah, a new leader, the son of Yonah Bogale, "we may lose all of our people."

The demonstrations made the newspapers, but the secret held. These mysterious demonstrators refused to talk about how they had arrived in Israel. There was strict censorship about the underground routes that their Ethiopian brothers and sisters were still following.

The first operation took place out of Addis Ababa, the sprawling capital city of Ethiopia. Menachem Begin—with his prickly manner, his demanding voice, his burning eyes—was the master planner. To Begin, the falashas were one of the most ancient communities in the Jewish diaspora. "We must bring them home," he said.

In 1977, on his first visit to Washington as prime minister, Begin had a long agenda. Egypt's President Anwar Sadat had made his dramatic visit to Jerusalem, and Begin was pursuing the possibility of peace.

He also wanted to talk about Ethiopia. It was part of an undercover bargain he hoped to strike with Lieutenant Colonel Mengistu Haile Mariam, the man who had emerged from the Marxist power struggle as head of Ethiopia's ruling Dergue.

In private conversations, Begin played the role of Ethiopia's friend at the American court. He urged then-President Jimmy Carter not to turn his back on Ethiopia and not to side solely with Somalia in their border wars. If the free world did not neglect Ethiopia, he argued, she might be lured from the Communist fold.

Colonel Mengistu was aware of these conversations, according to Moshe Gilboa of the Israeli Ministry for Foreign Affairs. In turn, the Israelis were hoping for a sign, some indication of a willingness to allow at least a few Jews to emigrate.

As he sat in a meeting with Carter at the White House, a communiqué arrived for Begin. It came, through indirect channels, from Mengistu. Watching Begin's face, an aide realized it was good news.

That August, an Israeli cargo plane landed at the Addis Ababa airport and unloaded its freight, mostly military spare parts. On the return trip, about sixty black Jews, mostly young people, filled the cargo bay. Nothing was said, nothing was written on the flight plan, but Ethiopia had agreed to turn a blind eye.

A few months later, a second plane landed and delivered its military goods. Then it, too, took off with its living contraband, another sixty black Jews.

Secrets are hard to keep in the Middle East. At a press conference, Moshe Dayan, then minister of defense for Israel, let it slip that Israel was trading military equipment for Ethiopian Jews. Begin was furious when he heard about the gaffe, but it was too late. Prodded by Soviet advisers who were hostile to Israel, Mengistu might have been waiting for an excuse to stop the planes.

A door that had been ajar was now slammed shut. It would not be the last time that the falashas would find themselves trapped because someone spoke out of turn.

The next exit routes that the Israelis tried led straight to calamity. In the late 1970s, according to reporter Louis Rapoport of the *Jerusalem Post,* two or three Ethiopian Jews left Israel and slipped back into Gondar province. Their plan was to load the back of a truck with bootleg passengers, then race south from the falasha villages, down the length of Ethiopia and across the border to Kenya. They were new at this game, and the operation floundered. A truckload of falashas were caught and arrested.

Then two Frenchmen were recruited, with an offer of five hundred dollars a head for every Jew they could deliver to Kenya. All that happened was more arrests.

Begin had set up an intergovernmental committee to work on this rescue, but the situation was becoming critical. Brought out of Ethiopia, Yonah Bogale was now a frail old man, but in November 1979 he traveled from Israel to Montreal, Canada, to ask a meeting of Jewish organizations for help. "Our final hour is near," he told them. "Until when shall we cry?"

Israel had been slow to hear the falashas' cry. Now she was doing what she could, but so far that had been very little. For some people, the black Jews of Ethiopia became confused with a group of former Black Muslims from America who called themselves "The Black Israelites." The group offended many people with their claim that they, not the other Israelis, were "the real Jews." By 1979, fourteen hundred of them had settled in a Negev town. That same year, Israel also provided a haven for a different, desperate group, four hundred boat people. It was a generous gesture, but it meant that there were now more Vietnamese refugees in Israel than there were Ethiopian Jews.

Only about three hundred Ethiopians had made it to Israel. Some had arrived on those contraband planes out of Addis. A small handful had left Ethiopia as legal exceptions—to seek medical treatment or to study. By ones and twos, others had come on foot, as stowaways on cargo ships, any way they could manage.

A delegation of those black Jews came to plead with Begin for the twenty-eight thousand who were still in Ethiopia. Among them was Rachamim Eleazar, tense, shadow-thin, with restless, graceful hands. Ten years earlier, a teenager walking barefoot across a desert, he had made his own way to Israel. He would always remember the words of this meeting.

"You are our brothers, our flesh and blood," Begin told them. "We will not let our brothers suffer." Yet, as the prime minister explained, he had no direct contact with the Ethiopian government. "We are doing what we can," he said, "but Ethiopia will not allow *aliyah.*"

"Then our people will make *aliyah* without permission."

"How?"

"Across the border, from a different country."

To consider the possibilities, Begin called in his aides. They spread the maps on the conference table and pondered them. The closest border was more than two hundred difficult, dangerous miles from the falasha villages.

It was Sudan, a member of the Arab League, a nation technically at war with Israel. Still, in that year, when only five falashas managed to reach Israel directly from Ethiopia, thirty-two had followed the Sudan route to freedom. Further, when Egypt signed the Camp David peace treaty with Israel, only two Islamic nations had not cursed and condemned President Anwar Sadat. One was tiny Oman. The other was Sudan, an African vastness the size of the subcontinent of India.

"There are mountains to cross, and a terrible wasteland," Begin said. "How can people make such a trek?"

"Our people can make it. When we talk about Jerusalem, our people will do it."

Begin nodded. "The government of Israel cannot push the people to go to Sudan," he explained. "But if they arrive there, we will take care of them."

Agents of the Mossad, the Israeli secret service, were already in place. The Mossad's secret weapon is its James-Bondish myth, its reputation for being everywhere and knowing everything. In Africa, there were Mossadniks under all sorts of guises and available in every color, white-skinned, brown, or black. There were whispers of British journalists in Sudan and Australian bushwhackers in Kenya. Cuban Jews were said to have infiltrated the ranks of Cuban "advisers" in Ethiopia. Other agents could be called in at a moment's notice from Egypt or Yemen. Ethiopians now in Israel could be smuggled back to Africa to help rescue their brothers.

Begin smiled. "We will find a way to bring those Jews here," he promised.

A few at a time, the Ethiopian Jews began to cross into

Sudan. It was a way station, a place to hide among the other refugees from famine and persecution until they could be moved farther along the road to Israel. Begin's promise was full of peril, but he and his successors—Yitzhak Shamir, himself a one-time Mossad chieftain, and Shimon Peres—tried to keep it.

In 1981, a sea route was opened. A curious convoy of trucks moved along the road from the refugee camp of Tawawa, not far from the border city of Gedaref. They lumbered northeast, to Port Sudan on the Red Sea. There, in a little-used section of the port, 350 black Jews clambered out of the trucks. Under cover of darkness, they were loaded into small boats. After a two-day sea voyage, they arrived at the Israeli port of Eilat.

Israeli gunboats patrolled that part of the Red Sea in those days. To avoid any mishaps, Israeli Navy frogmen had mapped the reefs off Port Sudan. The route worked well, with swift missile boats, landing craft, and speedboats used to ferry the illegal passengers. Once, even a submarine was pressed into service.

If any Sudanese noticed, some were well paid for their silence and others did not require money. The Sudanese had opened their hearts and their borders to a tidal wave of refugees, and they made no religious distinctions. They may have been anti-Zionist but, in Sudan at least, that was not always a code word for anti-Jewish.

Then, in March 1982, something went wrong. Three trucks had brought more than two hundred falashas to Port Sudan. As they were preparing to board the waiting boats, Sudanese soldiers appeared. Suddenly, they opened fire. As the falashas raced for the boats, the Israelis returned the barrage. In the shoot-out, a few falashas were captured, one was wounded, and the operation was dead in the water.

Another route was ready and waiting. Once a week or so, starting in 1980, a truck or van would drive up to the camps and load up with falashas. Political refugees, whose lives were in immediate danger, had first priority. Then it was on a "first come, first go" basis. A few people at a time, they made the five-hour drive to Khartoum, the capital city in the heart of Sudan. There, they waited in a safe house until they could be slipped aboard a plane to Athens or Paris.

For the drive from the refugee camps to Khartoum, they needed internal travel passes to get by the police roadblocks. To board the plane, they required exit visas. Somehow, sometimes through friendly contacts, often through bribery, Israeli agents acquired or forged the necessary travel documents for the refugees.

When things were going smoothly, about sixty people a week were rescued by this Khartoum route. At other times, in exits that were semilegal, the Jews were smuggled an even longer way around.

In the refugee camps, the United Nations High Commissioner on Refugees (UNHCR) would screen and assemble a group of scrawny, ragged travelers. A private relief agency would arrange the transportation from the camps to Khartoum. The Sudan Commission for Refugees provided the paperwork, a bloc visa that showed no names, only the number of people who would be permitted to leave.

To complete the escape, they had entry visas for Kenya and work permits—issued on the condition that they never be used. Kenya was south, the opposite direction from the promised land, but from there the refugees could be flown to a friendly country and then on to Israel. Sometimes, on the El Al plane that landed once a week in Nairobi, they could fly directly to Israel.

Now and then Christians and Moslems were plucked from the refugee camps and taken along this same route, all but the last stop. For them it was fully legal, and the work permits—for an African country, a Moslem one, or a nation in Western Europe—were meant to be used.

Different countries were willing to take different refugees as immigrants. The United States took some, especially those who had worked for American companies in Ethiopia, but America's quota was only three thousand a year from all of Africa. Canada was willing to take a few, but she preferred doctors, computer programmers, and other rare, highly skilled refugees. For her part, Sweden offered to take those who were physically handicapped. Each country had its own criteria, and so did Israel; she would take an entire group, anyone who was Jewish, young or old, sick or healthy, educated or not.

"Why should there be an obstacle to that?" wondered Jean-Claude Concolato, a spare, intense Frenchman who headed the UNHCR office in Gedaref. When he arrived in Sudan, though, he was warned against helping the falashas. "The warning was unclear, but many things in Sudan were unclear."

At first he ignored the warning. "The mandate of UNHCR is to protect refugees," he explained. "These people are in worse shape and greater danger than the others, so I have to protect them according to their needs."

In Sudan, there was a certain safety in vagueness. If a family was in a refugee hut one day and gone the next, the Frenchman tried not to notice. He did not want to know where they had gone. He did not want to hear the whispers about the Mossad. "That is not my business," he said.

The falashas were suspicious of the relief workers, and slow to trust anyone, white or black. One day, with nowhere else to turn, a desperate man came to Concolato's office. "A group of Jews have been caught on the road to Khartoum," the man explained. "They have no papers. They are in the jail."

Concolato hurried through the dusty, unpaved streets to the police station. "Why are you holding these people?" he demanded. "What's the charge?"

There were angry answers and loud arguments. Wrapped in his international authority, Concolato persisted. Eventually, he was allowed to lead the ragged and frightened lawbreakers back to the refugee camp.

After that, he was called on often to intervene. Sometimes,

when a large group was leaving, the falashas would alert him in advance. If they were stopped at a checkpoint or stranded when a truck broke down, he would be ready.

His discretion helped. So did his arithmetic. Food was distributed in "family units," barely adequate for a family of four or five, starvation for the large falasha families of nine or ten. "Look," he told them, "you must divide into two families, so you will have enough food."

He tried to be evenhanded. "If a few Christians are going to Europe, or Moslems are going to work in Saudi Arabia, I don't prevent them from going. So why should I prevent other people from going to other places? Just because they are Jews?"

He didn't always know who was a falasha and who wasn't; he only knew who needed help. In the screening process for scholarships in Western Europe, for medical visas and work permits, he tried to place the most vulnerable ones on the list. After a while, though, he learned to recognize the falashas. "Just in the way they stand," he explained, "you can see their terror."

Other people recognized them too. The falashas hunched down, trying to hide. Even when their numbers were small, they were different and conspicuous. Other refugees, especially their traditional enemies, the Amharic Christians, spotted them. When a few Jews were spirited out of the camp, the ones who remained were attacked and beaten by the other refugees. "We will stay here forever," one man shouted angrily. "Why should you have a place to go? If we are forgotten, why should you be remembered?"

After two years, the number of falasha arrests grew. Concolato was spending more and more time rushing to the police station. "I have a choice," he told an American visitor. "I can do nothing, but then I will lose my self-respect. Or I can do something, and get into trouble. The shame of this story is that some people think it is wrong to help."

The threats against his life became clear now and grave. The source was the fundamentalist Moslem Brothers—a faction that even President Nimeiry called "the brothers of Satan"— and it was time now for Concolato to leave Sudan. If his job was to protect refugees, he did it bravely. It did not help his career in refugee work, but there are people alive today who might have died without him.

Coolly, Israeli secret agents and American volunteers also risked their lives. Out of the camps, down midnight roads, they shepherded people to buses and trucks, boats and planes. In one small exodus after another, a dozen or two people at a time were saved.

"On a local basis, we can always save a few people," Yehuda Dominitz of the Jewish Agency explained matter-of-factly. His first rescue mission was to the Jews of Nazi Germany, and he has spent his life helping his brothers and sisters in distress. "A policeman can be bribed. A guard can fall asleep at the right time. We can always find a way."

Vaguely, the Sudanese knew that something was going on. In the offices of the state security service, a secret file was growing. In it they would place documents to show that they were making a determined effort to prevent foreign organizations from "smuggling out Jews." Other secret documents would complain that they lacked the men and resources to stop the illegal exits.

The operations were never simple or easy. Now and then there were echoes of the daring 1976 operation at Entebbe, when an Israeli plane swooped down on the Uganda airport to rescue hijacked airline passengers.

In mid-March of 1982, the insignia of the Israel Defense Forces were stripped from a C-130 Hercules transport. The unmarked plane landed on a makeshift field somewhere in the barren scrubland that stretched between Tawawa and Um Rakuba, the camps where most of the falasha refugees were huddled.

Truckloads of ragged, half-starved refugees were waiting.

When the cargo bay opened, an Israeli commando unit in full gear leaped out, rifles at the ready. "Hurry!" they ordered. As the refugees clambered on board, the soldiers spread out to guard the scene. Not a shot was fired. The landing and takeoff were made in darkness, synchronized for the time when the soldiers who manned the Sudanese radar system would be dozing at their posts.

Over the next two years there were half a dozen Hercules operations. Sometimes there was a single plane, sometimes a pair of them. Once there was a formation of three. All together, about thirteen hundred falashas were plucked from the Sudan desert and airlifted to Israel.

It ended in March 1984, when two unmarked planes landed illegally on the wasteland near the town of Shuwak. They left with a contraband cargo of hundreds of falashas. They were spotted by a desert nomad who reported the curious sight to the Sudanese police. The next day, the officers inspected the tracks left by Hercules C-130 transports.

The news of the secret planes spread. No one doubted that they were owned or leased by Israel. In Khartoum, in Washington, in Jerusalem, there were shudders. Borders do count for something; a nation cannot sit still while planes land illegally, without permission, even for humanitarian reasons. If another plane landed, if next time it were spotted sooner, seized or fired on, there would be repercussions.

Curiously, that danger had its advantages. The threat of an international incident loomed just as the number of falashas in Sudan was rising so quickly. It was clear to all the governments involved that something bolder was needed to remove the falashas from Sudan's territory.

What? How? When? No one knew yet, but eventually the answer would be Operation Moses.

## Chapter 8

# "The Name of the Other Is Pity"

MALKA ALEMIE MADE up her mind. It was the spring of 1984, and they had been walking out of Ethiopia for eight nights now, moving in the darkness through the mountains and forests, a weary and hungry caravan.

At daylight they stopped and hid among the trees. "Are we in Jerusalem yet?" little Tzion asked sleepily. Across the brown stretch of fields Malka could smell the cooking fires and see the grass roofs of a village.

Now she decided. She would ask—no, she would beg—for food. The children needed something more than dried chickpeas and water.

"It's dangerous," Josef, the guide leader, warned her. "I don't know that village." Rifle at the ready, he would wait. The village Christians might be friendly, or they might surround her with guns. They might send for government troops. "Then I cannot help you," Josef said. "I will have to run away with as many of your people as I can."

Malka nodded. "The children are hungry," she repeated.

Gaunt and determined, she walked across the fields toward the cluster of *tukuls.* Soon it would be planting time, and Malka wondered what sort of harvest this exhausted earth, cracked with dryness, would yield.

Unexpectedly, she felt embarrassed. "I look like a scarecrow," she thought. She no longer "smelled of water." Her dress was torn, and soiled with the dust of her journey. Straightening the fringed cloth that wrapped her head, she told herself, Don't be such an old fool.

A woman her own age stood in the doorway of a *tukul.* On her forehead was the faded blue tattoo of a cross.

"The little children are hungry . . ." Malka began.

The woman smiled. "Come in," she said. "You've traveled a long way." She asked no questions, but she insisted that Malka drink some coffee. "These are bad times," the woman sighed. "We don't have much." Then she poured milk into the jug Malka was carrying and wrapped food in a cloth.

"Go with God," the woman said. When Malka left, there were other Christians waiting outside. "If others are hungry," one of them called out, "send them."

Even near a friendly village, it was dangerous to stay in one place for too long. Yet it was Friday night, the eve of the Sabbath. "Let's go, let's go," the guides urged, but the falashas would not march. "We must keep the Sabbath holy," Malka explained. "If we forget we are Jews, why are we walking to Jerusalem?"

An elderly *kes* traveled with them, carrying a worn book, "the things of Moses." That evening and the next day, they gathered around him. In her prayers, Malka remembered the Christian woman. All of them remembered the prophecy of Isaiah: "*. . . and ye shall be gathered one by one, O ye children of Israel. . . . and they shall come which were ready to perish . . . and the outcasts . . . and shall worship the Lord in the holy mount at Jerusalem.*" (Isa. 27:12–13)

At sundown the caravan moved on, quiet and disciplined. Still limping and feverish from the wound on her leg, leaning heavily on her walking stick, Malka took each mile as a painful triumph.

Hours later, a sudden burst of automatic rifle fire shattered the night stillness. *"Shifta!"* the guide leader shouted. "Get down!" Once again Malka flung herself to the ground, clutching a grandchild, hugging the earth. Both sides had Kalashnikov rifles, made in Russia, picked up in skirmishes with government troops. This time, outnumbered by the guides, the *shifta* ran off.

The plateau of Ethiopia is split by deep gorges as it drops off toward Sudan. They struggled up the precipices and down. Sometimes, flattened against a rocky wall, terrified of falling into a bottomless pit, Malka could catch a whiff of the flowers that grew far, so far, below.

The caravan had become a village, and they improvised ways of helping each other. Some people had left their villages hurriedly, empty-handed, and those who had some food shared it. When it was safe to have a fire, the women took turns cooking for the group. One day, Eigal carried little Tzion on his shoulders so that a weary old man could take his place on the mule. Another day, the Alemies' mule balked and trembled, unable to carry its burdens for another mile. They packed the supplies and the two children onto other mules. Unburdened, perhaps their animal would survive another day.

Beyond the mountains, the land became flatter, and the days hotter. "Soon there will be no more villages," the leader told Malka. This day, though, they could smell the cooking fires.

A small, hopeful group of women approached the village. Perhaps they could fill the water jugs at the spring. Perhaps there was some food. A knot of villagers saw them coming and were waiting for them.

*"Ayud!"* a young man spat. It was an insulting Amharic word for "Jew," a synonym for the English word *kike*.

"You are going to the land of the *Ayud,"* someone yelled,

waving a stick. "Why should we give you anything? You should give *us* your animals and your money."

Angry shouts followed the women as they ran back to the caravan. Gasping, her heart pounding, Malka told the leader what had happened. "Pack up!" he shouted. "Move out!"

Already, one of the villagers could have gone for the government police. It was still daylight, but safer to go than to stay. "Hurry!" the guides shouted. They moved as quickly as they could, a ragged and stumbling file of exhausted people and worn-out animals, trying to put distance between themselves and the hostile village.

Malka strained to listen for the sounds of pursuers, but all she could hear was her own wildly beating heart and the gasping for breath of those around her. They pushed through the day and most of the night before they dared to rest. They waited, not knowing if they had been betrayed to the police or not. If anyone had been following, they seemed to have lost them.

They had reached the wasteland now. Malka called it "the desert that doesn't look like a desert." It was flat, with scrub growth, stunted trees, and coarse grasses that whipped their legs as they walked. They had come from the mild climate of the plateau, and the steamy heat of the wasteland made them stagger.

The hot wind carried unfamiliar, fetid smells. Lions lived here, and other wild animals. Now and then there was an unexpected noise, a sound of beasts on the prowl, and Malka stiffened at unseen dangers. What is more terrible? she wondered. The wild animals or the wild people?

Eigal shuddered. "I fear the things I can't see or hear," her son admitted. "The crawling things, the snakes."

In the dark, a barefoot teenager had stepped on a snake and been bitten. They had cut the wound and sucked out the poison, but he couldn't walk. "No one must be left behind," Malka commanded. Sometimes she didn't recognize her own voice.

She still wondered if anyone would listen to her. Yet they carried him, delirious, on a stretcher made of two tree limbs and strips of cloth.

When the sun was high, they rested. Even at night Malka could feel the heat of the ground through her sandals. Some people had no sandals, and their feet blistered.

Their canteens were almost empty, but the guides found one water hole after another dry. "Soon," the guides promised. "Soon."

At dawn, after the third night in this wasteland, there was a spring, gushing with fresh water. There, behind a clump of trees, another band of *shifta* waited for them. The first shots rang out. Once again the people scattered, flinging themselves to the ground. Malka pulled one of the little children from the mule and threw herself to the ground on top of him. In an answering volley, the guides aimed toward the trees.

How long before the firing stopped? Pressed against the earth, Malka thought two hours must have passed. Then the shouting started. When she understood the words, Malka gasped. Frightened, she looked around for Kohava and teen-aged Mazel. This time the *shifta* wanted more than money— they wanted the young women.

"You will kill us first," Josef shouted. "Or we will kill you." All that day, they laid siege to the water hole. As the sun was setting, the guide leader crawled along the ground, from one knot of people to another.

"We and they are old enemies," Josef whispered to Malka. "They will not back down. They will not give us the water."

When the night turned black, a signal was passed. "Keep low," the guides hissed. "Keep quiet." On their hands and knees, the people crawled out of range of the *shifta* guns.

They were weak with the heat, and dizzy with thirst. Only the guides still had water in the cans loaded on their mules. Once while the sun beat down, and again in the middle of the night's walk, they gave each child a small drink. "Mama, you must drink too," Josef told Malka, but she shook her head. "The children," she insisted through dry lips. "They are the ones we must save."

They were wandering through a graveyard. Their own animals were faltering, and they could see the skeletons of mules that had given out on other treks, their bones picked clean by hyenas and carrion birds. Then Malka shuddered. There were different bones, human ones.

For two nights they walked without water. Behind her, Malka heard a moan. She turned to see a man, a tattered skeleton really, stumble and fall. He lay unmoving on the ground, dead of heat and thirst. "Keep moving," the guides ordered, but they would not leave him for the vultures. In the wilderness, they dug a shallow grave for him and covered it with stones. "Hurry," the guides urged, but now there were prayers to say.

*"God will change heaven and earth like a garment . . ."* promised an old falasha prayer, a description of Judgment Day. The angel Michael *("his eye is that of a dove; his robe is of lightning")* would rise up and blow the trumpet on Mount Sinai. The pure would be separated from the unclean, and the angels would bring two sacrificial oxen, one from the east and one from the west. *"The name of the one is Grace and the name of the other is Pity."*

For another night, in a parched daze, they staggered on. Then the sky opened and there was a sudden rainstorm. They lifted their faces, open-mouthed to the welcome drops. They filled their canteens with water that collected in the crevices of rocks and the crooks of twisted trees.

In two more nights, they had passed through the wasteland and into a hillier countryside. Suddenly, in the distance, they heard the sound of hoofbeats. "Take cover!" the guide leader ordered. Crouched behind a knoll, scarcely breathing, Malka counted twelve armed men moving by, horses at a slow canter.

One horse stumbled, and Malka heard the weary rider swear. They were a cadre of the Tigrayan rebel army, and unpredictable. Sometimes, because they too hated the Dergue, they were friendly to the Jews. Other times, they were hostile. Idly, like a casual sightseer, one of the riders looked toward Malka's hiding place, and she pressed even closer to the earth until the troop had passed.

"We are coming close to Sudan," the leader announced the next day. They arrived at Wadi Kura and came face to face with a mirror image of themselves, another ragged caravan of Jewish refugees from Woggera.

As the Jews greeted one another, the guides began to quarrel. The Woggera guides were demanding money, from their own people and from Malka's group too. "No," Josef shouted. "You cannot take anything from these poor people."

"The Dergue are coming," a Woggera guide yelled. "Give us the money quick or you'll be captured."

Wildly, Malka looked around. Had they come this far to be captured? She heard the snap of ammunition clips being fitted into rifles. Then the familiar troop of guides surrounded their people, and they waited out the night.

By morning, there were still no government troops. It had been a lie, to scare the people. Yet Josef and his men still had their rifles at the ready, aimed now at the Woggera guides.

"We'll keep them here while the people go on," Josef said.

"We must say good-bye now, mama," he told Malka. It was one day's walk to the border, but the guides could go no farther. If the Sudanese soldiers saw them, they would confiscate their guns.

"You are a *baaltet.*" The leader smiled. "Just take your family straight. You will see three hills. Beyond them it is Sudan."

The two groups of refugees, now a weary army of five hundred, began to walk. Terror met them a few hours later at the three hills: another band of Tigray rebels. Too late to run and scatter, without guns to protect themselves, they waited to hear their fate.

"We are poor refugees," Malka tried to explain. Grimly, she wondered if her family had enough money left to buy the right to pass, perhaps the very right to live, from these soldiers.

"Don't worry, don't worry," a gruff rebel told her. As he talked, Malka began to smile with relief. The Tigrayan leader explained that they had been in Sudan. With his words, fear melted and Malka smothered a laugh. All they wanted was to change their money. "We'll give you Sudan money for Ethiopian *birr,*" he proposed. Gladly, still laughing, Malka exchanged the bit of money she still had.

In a few more hours, they were at a branch of the Atbara, the river that marks the border between Sudan and Ethiopia. We don't need the waters to part for us, Malka thought. There is no water. They walked across the dry riverbed to the other side.

The Sudanese soldiers who met them were bored now by the thousands of refugees who pushed into their country each day. Christians, Moslems, Jews, they all looked alike, ragged and hungry. Impatiently, they questioned them. "We are Christians," Malka lied, "running from the famine." Then Eigal produced the Sudanese money they'd just acquired, so the exhausted family could ride in a truck rather than walk the last twenty miles to the refugee camp.

An hour later, coming over one final hill, Malka could see the teeming acres of tents and mud huts that was the refugee camp of Um Rakuba. She shuddered. In the heat of Sudan there was the strange stench of old graves and new death. On a swampy plot of ground, a breeding place for malaria, they were still building *tukuls* for the flood of new refugees. As they dug, they uncovered the bones of people who had died here a thousand years earlier. Not far from this ancient graveyard, a new cemetery was growing to the size of a city.

It was May 1984, and Malka Alemie and her family had

arrived just in time for a crisis. That summer, food, medicine, and water would be scarcer than ever; disease would be epidemic.

"Are we in Jerusalem yet?" little Tzion asked again. After a trek of seventeen days and nights, they were still a long way from the promised land—and closer now to tragedy.

# Chapter 9

# *In the Footsteps of Moses*

IN JERUSALEM, they did not know Malka Alemie's name. Still, they knew what she, and so many others, had dared to do. And they knew what had to be done next.

A string of barrackslike buildings, pipe-rack plain, is home for the Foreign Ministry of Israel. Here, Moshe Gilboa offered a wry smile. "Nothing succeeds like success," the diplomat explained.

Between September 1983 and March 1984, Israeli agents had spirited almost all the falashas out of the Sudanese camps. They had expected more to follow from Ethiopia a few at a time. Instead, by the summer of 1984 there were more than ten thousand of them in Sudan.

Their desperate trek had changed everything. There were too many to hide now in refugee camps that were short on food and long on death. There were far too many to smuggle out along the secret routes of the Mossad.

A larger-scale operation was urgently needed. To make that happen in Sudan, the Israelis knew, they would need the cooperation and help of the United States.

In March and April 1984, there were a number of State Department meetings to discuss the situation in Sudan. Among those taking part were Richard Krieger, then assistant coordinator of Refugee Affairs; Princeton Lyman, then deputy assistant for East Africa; Elliott Abrams, then assistant secretary for Human Rights; Arthur Dewey and James Purcell of the Agency for International Development (AID).

The United States had a stake in Sudan and a certain amount of leverage there. Sudan's strategic position on the Red Sea made her a security concern for the United States. Sudan's friendship with Egypt was a plus for American policy in the area. Her other neighbors—Ethiopia's Marxists to the south and Libya's Khadaffi in the west—were a worry.

Because of these concerns, Sudan had been receiving more U.S. aid than any other African nation except Egypt. Beyond those hundreds of millions, because of America's humanitarian interest in the teeming refugee camps, the United States was providing 35 to 40 percent of the UNHCR budget and sending still more help through food-surplus programs and the AID bureau.

The meetings continued through the spring. The State Department men were frustrated. Each new report on the falashas contradicted the one before it. One day, there would be grim news from the AAEJ, reports of human disaster and mass death. The next day, there would be a cable from Jerry Weaver, America's refugee officer at the Khartoum embassy, telling of fewer difficulties and cutting back the death toll from thousands to hundreds. There were reports from Israeli sources, too, falling somewhere in between.

Months later, Krieger would learn that his best source of information had been the AAEJ, the group he called "the crazies." In a private meeting, face to face with Weaver at last, he would hear the Khartoum officer admit that he had downplayed the disaster. As Weaver explained, he'd sent a wrong, falsely low death count; he had believed that little, if anything, could be done about the situation, and he didn't want to excite people or encourage further risky free-lance rescues by the AAEJ. For some of the same reasons, according to Krieger, the Israelis had put a gloss on their own reports.

For now, Richard Krieger was growing angry and impatient. He fired off an order to Jerry Weaver: "Get down there and see what's going on."

Weaver was on his way. He'd already had a visit from a distraught man, a Swedish nurse from Um Rakuba who cried—"literally wept"—over the falashas who were trapped there.

Weaver saw for himself. The spring rains had turned the grounds into a muddy sewer. He found the falashas huddled ten or twelve to a hut, sick and starving, afraid to use the few medical facilities the camp had, too terrified even to visit the open fields that had been set aside as outdoor toilets. The sanitary conditions were appalling. The figures he collected on falasha disease and death were "incredible."

The case histories he heard were terrible. Food was scarcer than ever. Hungry, looking for a scapegoat, some of the Amhara refugees had turned on the Jews with growing violence. Falashas were being attacked, driven out with brutal words and blows, their pathetic huts burned down.

The embassy had "discretionary funds," and Weaver was able to get some of that money released for emergency aid. He set up meetings with UNCHR in Khartoum. Finally, he reported the grim truth to Washington.

Krieger and others at the State Department hoped for a falasha rescue. But they were clear on one thing: The American government could not take part in a selective rescue. They could not favor the Jews over any other group, but they could make the choice that was most reasonable and most feasible. They could throw a lifeline to the people who were closest to drowning, the ones in greatest danger, the only ones with a place to go.

In Sudan, that was the falashas. The United States had a

humanitarian concern here, as with millions of other refugees around the world. Beyond that, the United States had little to gain from a falasha rescue, and a great deal to lose. In the geopolitical puzzle, Sudan was a key piece. Her friendship was important, and so were the "sensitivities" of other Arab nations. The Americans would have to proceed with caution.

As the men at the State Department realized, a rescue could happen only with the consent, however tacit, of the Sudanese government. Yet that country had made its anti-Israel position clear. The words of Gaafar al-Nimeiry, president of Sudan for sixteen years, were blunt but true: "Israel knows I am its enemy."

On a morning in mid-June of 1984, Richard Krieger, a low-key diplomat with deep-set, brooding eyes, ushered an official visitor from Sudan into his office. Because publicity could cost this man his current government job, and even his life, we will guard his identity as Mr. "X."

The visitor wanted more American aid for Sudan. He ticked off his country's long list of problems—the economy in shambles, the uneasy borders, the rising flood of refugees.

As he listened, Krieger had a flash of hope. "And on top of that, those Jews," the man was saying angrily, "always making trouble."

Krieger nodded, his expression neutral. To himself, he thought, Hey, this guy doesn't like Jews. He believes all the old lies. I can use that.

When the meeting was over, Krieger hurried across the hall to test his new idea on his boss, Ambassador H. Eugene Douglas. "I've found an opening," Krieger argued, excited now. "I know how to sell this guy on letting the Jews go."

Gene Douglas agreed that it was worth a try. Quickly, the idea was cleared with Chester Crocker, head of the African Bureau, and with Hume Horan, the ambassador in Khartoum. With this go-ahead, Krieger invited Mr. X to return to the State Department that same afternoon.

Krieger, Douglas, and Mr. X met in the ambassador's office, all brown woods and leather, a map of the world the only spot of color. Carefully, Krieger began.

"You're right," he pretended to sympathize. "You don't need those Jews making trouble for you. We'd like to help you find a way to get all of them out of your country."

He dangled the advantages. It would be a relief to have ten thousand fewer mouths to feed. If the falashas were gone, it would end the threat of those unmarked planes landing in the desert. If they went, "the crazies" would be gone too.

He played on the man's prejudices. "You know how Jews stick together," he said, "and you know the power of American Jews."

Krieger and Douglas didn't dare look at each other. Here was Krieger, a Jew himself, mouthing all the hateful stereotypes. It was a crude approach, but it seemed to be working. "You know they control everything," Krieger was saying, "the banks, the media, the Congress."

Mr. X was smiling, and Krieger felt encouraged. He lured the man on. "If Sudan wants more American aid, you'll need my Jewish friends on Capitol Hill. Think what they could do for your country if they thought you were helping these people get out."

Eventually, aid to Sudan grew by $50 million, for a total of $250 million for fiscal year 1985. The U.S. government still insists that the increased aid was not a payoff for Sudan's cooperation in a falasha exodus. Yet as Krieger would say later, "I wasn't sitting across from Raoul Wallenberg [the brave Swedish diplomat who saved so many Jewish lives during the Holocaust]. There had to be something in it for Sudan."

As he promised that day, "I'll help you. I'll pass the word. I'll make Sudan look like the great humanitarian country it is."

Mr. X seemed to like the idea. He would check with his government—"with Vice-President Tayeb," Krieger guessed— and get back to them. When the Sudanese had gone, Krieger and Douglas beamed at each other. "He's hooked," Krieger gloated. "We've made the initial sale."

The next day, Mr. X reported that the first reaction was favorable. "We'll meet in Geneva during ICARA [International Conference on African Relief Assistance] and I'll have a final answer."

Krieger was flying. Sudan was about to say yes to a secret exodus of the Jews. Yet there was still no plan, only a principle—that the United States would help to make such an exodus happen.

A memo outlining the concept of a falasha rescue was sent to President Ronald Reagan and Secretary of State George Shultz. Quickly, an answer came back: "Approved."

Krieger was now dispatched to Jerusalem to brief the key Israelis. Among those he saw on this trip were Yehuda Dominitz of the Jewish Agency and Moshe Gilboa of the Foreign Ministry. On July 7, he flew from there to Geneva, where Gene Douglas and Mr. X were waiting.

The Sudanese had good news. His government had agreed to the exodus—with details to be worked out later.

At the request of the Israelis, Krieger raised another issue with Mr. X in Geneva. While they worked out a plan, could Sudan ease up on "certain avenues" that the Israelis were using to move a few Jews at a time out of Sudan?

"What avenues?" Mr. X asked, leaning forward, suddenly curious. Krieger's mouth went dry. Had he let a secret out? Then he saw the man smile. "All right," Mr. X agreed. "We already know what they are." Over the next months, Israel was able to increase the flow of smuggled Jews.

The Israelis were keeping a low profile, but they were not idle. They were exploring every possibility, pulling every string they could. If they couldn't talk directly to Sudan, they were searching for other people who could carry a message.

They found unexpected friends who encouraged Nimeiry to

smile and say yes. "A third country," according to a high-level Israeli official, "an ally from the Communist world," was helpful in this and other ways. By other whispers, so was Adnan Khashoggi, the Saudi Arabian billionaire, the ubiquitous arms dealer who would later be involved in the Irangate affair. Khashoggi is rumored to have mediated between Israel and Sudan, playing a vital part in winning Nimeiry's tacit agreement to a falasha airlift.

Nimeiry cared deeply about his image in the Arab world, and Egyptian leaders also were helpful on this score. They reassured him that he would not be "a traitor" to his fellow Arabs if he allowed the Ethiopian Jews to leave his refugee camps. As they reminded him, he did not need to be "more Arab" than Iran or Iraq, Morocco or Yemen, all Moslem nations who had let many of their Jews go.

Yet the Sudanese were nervous. As they warned again and again, they would have to come up with a plan that would not embarrass Sudan in the Arab world. At this point, it was up to General Omar el-Tayeb, vice-president and head of state security, and President Nimeiry, and Mr. X bowed from the scene.

The two Niles, the Blue and the White, come together in Khartoum, a sprawling city of 2.5 million people. East and West meet here too, a Hilton hotel towering over dusty streets, bustling and crowded with the colorful costumes of Africa and the caftans of Arabia. In the swelter of this desert capital, Ambassador Hume Horan and refugee officer Jerry Weaver began a series of meetings with Tayeb and two Sudanese colonels.

"Horan was heroic. He stuck his neck out. He refused to give up," Krieger said later. "If Horan had said no, that would have been it. If Gene Douglas had said no. Or George Shultz. Or Ronald Reagan." Before Reagan appointed him to the State Department, Krieger had been president of the Federation of

Jewish Organizations. He was forever grateful to "the righteous gentiles" who said yes.

As they talked in Khartoum, Horan knew that people were dying. Under a tidal wave of human misery, the refugee system broke down, and there were fatal shortages of food and medicine. Exhausted by their trek, the falashas were weaker, sicker, dying at a faster rate than anyone else.

They met again and again. All summer, a workable plan seemed to elude them. Then, in September, the American diplomats in Khartoum were talking once more to their Sudanese counterparts.

"If only we could turn this problem over to someone else," a Sudanese leader said. He sighed, a man yearning to be rid of a burden.

The words hung in the air. The American envoy shifted in his chair; something clicked in his mind. Then the Sudanese leader finished his thought. "Why can't we find a refugee organization to take them off our hands?"

Why not? the American thought. His voice calm, his face a diplomatic mask, he promised to check it out with Washington.

"*That's it!*" In mid-September, excitement ran high at the State Department. They passed the cable from Khartoum from one excited hand to another. It was the "cover" they'd been looking for. Grinning, they told each other, "That's it. That's the answer!"

At last, Operation Moses was under way.

Finally, they had a face-saving formula. An international refugee organization would be responsible for the destiny and destination of the falashas. Technically, that relieved the Sudanese of further responsibility. A major function of such organizations was moving people in distress, transferring them from a place where they weren't wanted to a place where they were. They'd done it before, in Bangladesh and other countries, and they could do it again.

Yet this time it would be harder. "It must be done in secret," the leaders of Sudan insisted. Thousands of people would have to be moved long distances without anyone noticing. There could be no whispers, no rumors, no leaks.

It was up to Sudan to choose a refugee organization, one they could trust, out of dozens of groups who were operating in Sudan. Even now, because there may be other people to be rescued from other places in the future, the group's name cannot be revealed.

In the aftermath of this rescue, three refugee groups were expelled from Sudan for "smuggling Jews"—the Joint Voluntary Agency, the International Catholic Migration Commission, and the Intergovernmental Committee for Migration. All that can be said is that not all of them were "guilty" of this good deed.

The rescue was agreed on now. The rest was strategy—but not simple.

"Our part in this is to be the enablers and facilitators," Krieger explained. Yet in this rescue, that meant playing a risky and heroic role.

At the U.S. Embassy in Khartoum, Ambassador Horan nodded to refugee officer Jerry Weaver. He would be the point man. A burly, bearded man, Weaver was middle-aged, with a macho temperament. At times he made his bosses nervous. A one-time football player at Ohio University, he was independent and outspoken, "a hip-shooter," as a State Department official called him. He had a habit of making up the rules as he went along, and this time that made him the right man for a dangerous job.

Weaver became the American connection on an informal planning-and-operations team that included a Sudanese security expert and workers from the international refugee organization. Every detail had to be plotted, every contingency planned for. How would the people be moved? When? Along what route?

On a map, the simplest route was obvious. It was the sea

route that the Mossad had already tested. In a few hours, the Ethiopian Jews could be taken by buses or trucks to Port Sudan. From there, boats could travel up the Red Sea to Israel. For Sudan, that route was too direct to "enemy" territory.

The planning team mapped out a different route, one the Mossad had used so often. They would move the refugees overland to Khartoum, and by air from there to "a third country." Because a fleet of planes would attract too much attention, they would have to settle for one planeload at a time.

The largest number of falashas, Malka and her family among them, were in the sprawling camp of Um Rakuba. Yet the place was too busy with relief workers, police, and other visitors for a clandestine operation. If anything went wrong, there was no place to hide in the tiny village on its outskirts. For Weaver and the others, a better place to begin was Tawawa, a smaller camp just minutes outside of Gedaref.

The plan was to liberate the Jews at Tawawa, then filter in other Jews from other camps to this jumping-off point. Terrified and suspicious of strangers, the falashas could be found and gathered up only by someone they knew and trusted. In his head, Weaver was making a checklist of jobs that needed to be done. This one belonged to the Israelis; the Mossad had undercover agents already in place, and one or two Ethiopian Jews would be sent from Jerusalem.

Four busloads of people, they calculated, would fill a plane. They would need other sturdy vehicles to escort the buses, and security officers to protect them.

Only one good road ran between Gedaref and Khartoum. It was potholed and booby-trapped with police checkpoints. They would have to get past the police without giving away the secret. On the job list, this was Sudan security's problem.

They would need an isolated strip at the Khartoum airport, as far from the passenger terminal as possible. If anything went wrong, if a plane was late or a bus broke down, if the secret got out, they would need safe houses large enough to hide two hundred or so people. Weaver grinned. "That one's easy." The Americans already had a house in Gedaref that embassy people and their friends used on visits to the area. The Sudanese security had their own hideaway in Khartoum. All that was needed was to stock the safe houses with food and water.

Where would the planes come from? Where would they fly to? Weaver and his team had worked out a strategy for on-the-ground movements in Sudan. Now the policy makers would have to approve the scheme and devise other plans for what happened beyond Sudan's borders.

Where would the money to get the rescue off the ground come from? In Washington, Krieger huddled with Robbie Sabel, his liaison at the Israeli embassy. They calculated that it would cost $5 million to $7.5 million to lease and operate the planes they needed. The airborne rescue would be only the smallest part of the total bill. The cost for the first year of resettling these people—food, housing, education, and health care—would be twenty-five thousand dollars per person.

Yet Israel, mired in economic crisis, did not have the funds readily available for the planes, and it was too soon, too secret, to turn to the United Jewish Appeal (UJA), the fund-raising arm of the American Jewish community.

Once again, Krieger found a way. "The United States government may be able to help," he suggested. "It's unusual, but not *that* unusual." As he explained, the U.S. government had provided money for the movement of desperate refugees in the past. They had helped to create and to fund an international organization for this very purpose. There was also the president's Emergency Refugee Fund. On a number of occasions, on the advice of officials at the State Department or the National Security Council, the president had used this discretionary fund to help individuals or governments.

Word was passed to the Jewish Agency, which then cabled an appeal to Gene Douglas and George Shultz. Douglas discussed it with Krieger and then sent his recommendation to the

White House. At Douglas's urging, President Reagan agreed to make up to $5 million out of his emergency fund available for the falasha flights to freedom.

At last, on October 8, 1984, high-level representatives from the United States, Sudan, and Israel were on the neutral ground of Geneva, Switzerland. It was the first time they had all been in the same city for the same purpose, but Sudan and Israel still could not meet face to face.

In short-distance shuttle diplomacy, Richard Krieger, Jerry Weaver, and other Americans moved between the two hostile delegations—the security officers and colonels of Sudan and the Israelis from the Foreign Ministry, the Mossad, and the Jewish Agency. They met in office-building conference rooms and hotel bedrooms. They tried to keep the meetings small—"not a lot of people but still too many," said a worried Israeli official.

Here, Jerry Weaver unveiled the Khartoum plan. This guy is a cowboy, an Israeli official thought. He was uneasy with Weaver's macho bluster and the bravado images of midnight bus rides and mystery planes coming and going. If the Mossad were running it, the Israeli thought, I'd feel better. Yet as they talked, Weaver had an answer for every question. This man can do it, the Israeli decided. He can make the plan work.

The plan was sealed. In other meetings, on a need-to-know basis—the fewer people the better—they filled in the missing pieces.

At Krieger's insistence, Nicolas Morris, head of UNHCR in Sudan, flew to Geneva for one of the meetings. People were dying in the refugee camps, and Krieger wanted to know why the refugee system had broken down so badly. He was stunned to hear that, in a curious way, they had almost planned to be unprepared. They had been warned that a flood of new refugees—between 150,000 and 200,000 Christians, Moslems, and Jews—was on the way, but they had underestimated the numbers. They had decided *not* to stockpile food and medicines, because they worried that those supplies would be a "magnet" for still more refugees. Tight-lipped but still polite, Krieger told them to get the food and medicine delivered—and quickly.

Two sets of arrangements were worked out. Within its borders, Sudan was concerned with every detail of moving the refugees from the camps to the airport. Until now these people had been the responsibility of the Sudan Commission for Refugees. Now, for a secret operation, it was up to the Amnul Dawla, the state security organization that Vice-President Omar el-Tayeb presided over.

Beyond her borders, it was, as Sudan said, "not our problem." The planes could come to Khartoum from anywhere except Israel, flying any other flag. The Israelis nodded. It would be simpler to use their own airline, El Al, or their air force, but they knew how to find different planes. Both the Israelis and the Americans kept silent on one thing—the source of the money for the planes. As Krieger said later, "That was never Sudan's business."

Where would the planes fly to? Sudan was adamant that they must touch ground outside of Israel. As a point of logistics, Israel argued for direct flights. Then, reluctantly, the Israelis agreed. Discreetly, they would inquire about hospitable landing places in friendly countries. "We don't like it," explained a frequent traveler to Geneva, Yehuda Dominitz of the Jewish Agency, "but we've done it before."

Sudan was in a hurry, for secrecy's sake, and so was Israel, for her own reasons. "You never know what will happen," said Yehuda Dominitz. "The person who can be saved today should not be left for tomorrow." Many of the Israelis at these meetings were Orthodox, observant Jews, but they agreed that the planes could fly on the Sabbath.

On the ground in Sudan, Israel would have to be invisible. No one doubted, though, that her agents would be present and active.

In theory, this was a legal operation. In reality, they had to plot it and carry it out as if it were covert and outside the law. If word got out, everything would stop.

A jubilant group of Americans flew out of Geneva. If all went well, the first plane would take off in a matter of weeks. Yet Jerusalem was a rumor mill, and so was Khartoum. Washington often leaked like a sieve.

"Can we keep the lid on this one?" asked a worried American. Suddenly, the smiles faded.

"We had better," Krieger answered grimly.

# Chapter 10

# "The Answer Is Yes"

*"MY MOTHER IS CRYING,"* Gideon told the captain. "She wants to see me." One more time, he wanted to go home to Ethiopia, and his Sudanese friend provided the travel pass to the border.

The scrawny young spy was working for the Israelis now. One night, as he left his AAEJ friend on a narrow street in Gedaref, another Ethiopian had called to him from the shadows.

"Gideon?" He stared into an unfamiliar face. "I've been watching you," the stranger said. Gideon tensed, ready to move quickly, but the man's firm hand was on his shoulder. "Don't be nervous. I just want to talk. I have some work for you. Important work."

"What kind of work? Who are you?"

The man smiled. "A friend of Israel."

There was no mention of Mossad, but Gideon understood who the mysterious agent worked for. There were no credentials to prove it, but Gideon could check the man's identity with a mutual friend. The man gave him messages to deliver, sometimes in Ethiopia, sometimes inside the camps. On other dark

101

nights, Gideon would shepherd a group of falashas through the Gedaref alleyways he knew so well, to a rendezvous outside of town. Here, undercover Israeli agents waited to take them farther along the road to Jerusalem.

Gideon also became one of the "list makers." When Malka Alemie and her family arrived at Um Rakuba, for example, Gideon added their names to his list. His new bosses wanted to keep track of who the Jews were and where.

Gideon could guess why. Sometimes they gave him small amounts of money to distribute to the people. In the wretched camps and nearby towns, the falashas, sick and hungry, bartered for survival. Often, it was the price of some milk for a child or some quinine for an old man.

Yet it was more than that. Often, Gideon hitched a truck ride to the border to help new arrivals make their way to the camps. In May, a thousand falashas limped into Sudan in just two days. Between March and August 1984, almost twelve thousand of them were crowded into Um Rakuba. They were arriving by the thousands, but, as Gideon knew, they were dying by the hundreds. Israel had to know that. Something had to happen soon.

Before it did, he had one more trip to make, to smuggle a special person out of Ethiopia. "Esther," he sighed. He smiled at the memory of a graceful young woman with a sweet promise in her smile and corn-row braids in her hair. At nineteen, she was one of the "old virgins," as they called a new breed of Ethiopian girl who was allowed to go to school instead of being married off as early as age twelve.

Gideon had never spoken to her, and he had glimpsed her only twice, on his last trip. Yet that was twice more than many Ethiopian grooms saw their brides. Had she returned his gaze? Had she asked people about him, as he had about her? Gideon wasn't sure, but he had decided he would take her out of Ethiopia—as his wife.

The trip began badly. Crossing into Ethiopia, Gideon climbed the familiar three hills. They seemed steeper than he remembered. His limbs were aching and weary.

The malaria, he thought, it's coming back. He had not escaped the diseases of the refugee camps, but he couldn't stop now. Shivering with chills and fever, he pushed on through the night.

At dawn, he pulled himself up into the arms of a large tree, to hide and try to rest. He dreamed that he was running, pursued by a faceless enemy. All that he could recognize was the man's gun, a Kalashnikov.

With a start, he awoke to the sound of rough voices and the smell of coffee. A troop of soldiers had made camp nearby. Ethiopians, he thought, as the wind carried the Amharic words to him. If he climbed higher, he would be able to see whether the uniforms were government troops or rebels still loyal to Haile Selassie. Afraid that they might hear the creak of a limb or the rustle of leaves, he hid, unmoving, his legs cramping, until they left.

Stiff and weary, he forced himself to go on. At the end of that night's march, there should be a stream that might have water.

August, the cold, wet season of Ethiopia, was almost over. As Gideon walked, it rained, drenching him but also filling the stream. He was moving toward it when a large, tawny animal crossed ahead of him. Gideon and the lion spotted each other at the same moment, and both stopped in their tracks.

"Stay still!" a man's voice hissed from behind him. "If you move, he'll kill us both." Gideon had never seen a lion before, and he yearned to run. Heart pounding, he obeyed the voice. An eternity of terror passed. For ten minutes, man and beast stared at each other. Then the lion moved toward the stream and began to drink.

Now Gideon turned to see where the voice came from. Recognizing the man lying flat on the ground, he stifled a shout.

It was Josef, the Christian guide he'd met on his first flight from Ethiopia, the "honest bandit" he'd recommended to Malka Alemie.

When the lion had finished drinking and loped off, they embraced. Happily, they filled their water cans and agreed to travel on together.

Still tired and feverish, Gideon tried to keep up with his friend. After a few hours, he had to rest. Shivering in the August dampness, he retched a vile green fluid. "My head is dizzy," he said. "I don't know who I am."

Despite the danger, Josef built a fire to keep his friend warm. As Gideon slept, the nightmare returned: Someone was chasing him, trying to kill him, and there was no escape. Gideon's limbs thrashed wildly, and Josef tied his arms with his belt. In his sleep, Gideon was raving and crying out, and Josef held his head in his lap, a hand over his mouth.

When he awoke, the nightmare and the fever seemed over. The friends began to make their way across the wasteland. Three days later, they came to a crossroads.

"This is the way," Gideon said. "Gondar is east, toward the sun."

"No," Josef insisted. "The other way is shorter."

They argued, but neither stubborn man would give in. In angry silence, they divided the food and water, and each man went his own way.

For half the night, Gideon walked alone. Fool! he told himself, You've lost a good friend.

In the quiet night, he heard footsteps gaining on him. It was the sound of his nightmare, and he hid behind a tree. When the footsteps caught up, it was Josef.

"You are wrong about the road," the bandit growled. He seemed embarrassed. "Well, you are my friend," he muttered. "If you are sick, I cannot let you go on alone."

Together, they moved through the wasteland and into the Gondar hills. By the time they arrived at a village where one of Josef's uncles lived, Gideon was ill again, nauseous and trembling with fever.

To cure him, they used an ancient remedy, bloodletting. With a sharp knife, they made small cuts on Gideon's body, then placed heated glass cups to suction out the "bad blood." To Gideon, the blood looked black and poisonous.

The next day he felt lightheaded, but he was strong enough to sit up and talk to visitors, two Jews from a nearby village. "Are you going to Dembia?" one of the visitors whispered. "We want to go there, too." Uneasy, afraid someone might overhear, he used the falasha code word for Jerusalem. A man could disappear in remote, uninhabited Dembia; the police could search and never find him.

Gideon smiled. "Be ready in two weeks and I will take you to Dembia."

Dreaming of Esther, Gideon was impatient. A night later, he and Josef started to walk again, but after a few hours, weakened by the loss of blood, Gideon collapsed. Josef was cradling him in his arms, trying to stop the trembling, when a young Moslem found them.

"Come home with me," the boy insisted. He and Josef carried Gideon to a small *tukul*. Close to the fire, his parents made a pallet of blankets for Gideon, then wrapped him in still more blankets. When he awoke, they offered food and hot tea. Gideon reached for the clay mug, but his hand fell back feebly. The mother held it for him as he drank.

When he awoke again, Josef was watching over him. "Don't sit and suffer here with me," Gideon said. "Go along."

When Josef refused, Gideon had another idea. "My friend," he smiled weakly, "maybe you will arrange my wedding." His father was now in a distant village, but Gideon had an uncle living just one day's walk away. Perhaps Josef could carry a message, telling Gideon's uncle to visit the village of Esther's family.

"That is our custom," he explained. "My family must visit

her family, to ask for the daughter. Tell him I want no dowry. Listen, my friend, Esther is the only gift I ask for."

"I will be back with the answer," Josef promised. He grinned at his friend, huddled in blankets. "If the family is willing, I will dance at your wedding."

For most of the following days, Gideon slept. When he awoke, he remembered the conversation with Josef as a dream. The Moslem family found some quinine for him, nursed him, even slaughtered and cooked a hen for him.

In Ethiopia, Jews and Moslems are both minorities, sometimes friends and sometimes not. In Gideon's village, when the Amharic Christians moved the market day to Saturday, to taunt the Jews, a Moslem neighbor had helped. He'd acted as middleman for Gideon's father, selling his metalcrafts for him. At school, Gideon had fought with some Moslems, but one of them had told him, "You feel like my brother."

Politely, this family hadn't asked about Gideon's religion, and he wasn't sure if they'd guessed he was a falasha. "They would take care of me, Jew or not," he decided. "These are good people."

As his head cleared, Gideon grew worried. "How long has my friend been gone?" he asked the mother.

"Six days," she answered. Gideon feared for his friend. Going to his uncle's house or coming back, had he been captured?

"Mama," he told the Moslem woman, "I must go now too."

"Stay longer," she urged him. "Be our son and stay a year."

Gideon shook his head. "I will never forget you," he vowed. He embraced the Moslem family, quick kisses on each cheek, and then he moved on.

Two miles down the road, a horse was galloping toward him. The rider waved wildly. "Yes!" Josef was shouting. "The answer from Esther is yes!"

Two days later, Gideon, Josef, and the uncle started out for Esther's village. Normally, a falasha wedding took months to prepare for and a week or more to celebrate. They would follow all the traditions, but speeded up, everything telescoped by a time of crisis.

Family and friends had gathered for the wedding feast. They would be hungry next week, but today there was a roast sheep, *injera,* and dark, heady glasses of *tala.* The three men were led to places of honor. A drum and a homemade banjolike instrument played a pulsing African rhythm.

*"Addis Ababa, Addis Ababa,"* the men sang. The name of Ethiopia's capital, it meant "New Flower." To the black Jews, it was a song they sang at weddings and births, a chant of new hope and a hymn to God. The men danced to it—shoulders shrugging and swiveling, legs leaping quickly back and forth, heads pecking. In a mime of strutting roosters, the dancing grew in frenzy. Hands on shoulders, like wings, in an ecstasy of advancing and retreating, they dared each other on to dizzier spins and higher leaps.

Esther, the liberated young student, was playing the role of a traditional bride. She was nowhere to be seen as they ate and danced. Finally, at a signal from the *kes,* she was led from the *tukul.* Her face was hidden by a veil, her head bowed demurely.

A wedding guest carried a ceremonial umbrella—a festive curve of red silk, its edges elaborately embroidered—for the *kes.* The white-turbaned priest chanted verses from the Torah. Then Esther and Gideon exchanged promises to be a faithful wife and a good husband. A red-and-white band was tied around Gideon's forehead, a symbol of the bride's virginity and the groom's purity.

As the bride was led away again, the feasting and dancing continued. In normal times it would go on for days. Now it would last only through the night. In the morning, Esther emerged, swathed in a white *shamma* so that only her wide, dark eyes were visible.

Gideon pushed Josef forward. "Go, go," he said. "It's tradition." The bride was leaving home and family, and the groom's best friend was now supposed to become her special protector.

Gideon beamed at the bony, swaybacked horse that waited for his bride. He'd borrowed the poor animal to impress Esther's family. "If a man has a horse, he's rich," he explained to Josef. "And that means he must be a *shmagla,* a wise man."

With a wink for his friend, Josef lifted the bride onto the horse and walked at her side on the road back to the uncle's house. "If we didn't have a horse," Gideon said, laughing, "you'd have to carry her on your shoulders." Traditionally, they would have sung and danced along the way, but in these troubled times they walked quietly.

At his uncle's house, another feast awaited them. Esther was led away to a bridal *tukul,* a hut specially decorated for a wedding night. There was more singing and dancing.

Then Esther reappeared. Still veiled, she sat next to Gideon, still wearing his red-and-white headband. A *kes* said more prayers for them, and they repeated their promises and signed a marriage contract.

As the celebration went on, the bride and groom slipped away to the wedding *tukul.* Here, the bride was unveiled at last. Here, they touched, hands, mouths, bodies, for the first time.

Later, Gideon returned to the celebration. If the bride were not a virgin, the groom would tear off the headband, an announcement that he was discarding the bride as well. Grinning triumphantly, Gideon kept his headband.

Their honeymoon would be a trek to Sudan. A few days later, Gideon's uncle loaded a mule with water cans and more food than he could spare. Then he gave Gideon and Esther a special gift: two hard-to-get pieces of paper, the passes that were required to travel from one village to another. "At least your journey will start without trouble," he said.

After only a few hours, though, the ground shook. A troop of sixty armed men galloped toward the young couple and then reined to a stop. The troop was led by two peasant leaders, men elected by the local farmers to carry out the Dergue's orders.

"Where is your pass?" the first leader demanded. "Where are you going?"

"Armachiho." Gideon mumbled the name of a nearby village and handed over the passes.

"They are Jews," the first leader guessed, "and troublemakers." Unable to read, he handed the passes to the second leader. "Here, you check these."

Gideon and the second leader stared at each other, and a flicker of surprise passed between them. Gideon recognized the man as an old neighbor, a man who often drank beer with his father. The peasant leader remembered Gideon and could guess where he was headed.

He can betray me, Gideon thought, waiting tensely. The second leader studied the passes carefully and announced, "They are in order."

"They are Jews," the first leader still insisted. "I say we should take them to jail, passes or not."

"If they have passes, Jew or not, they must be allowed to go," the second leader shouted. He fingered the rifle on his shoulder. Gideon stared. Did the man wink quickly at him? Or was he only squinting in the sun as he proclaimed, "That is socialism!"?

When the first leader continued to protest, the second one led the newlyweds through the line of soldiers. When they were through, he leaned down from his horse and grabbed Gideon's shoulder. "Why do you come here?" he whispered. "Do you want to die? You must go and keep on going."

In the grove of trees near Armachiho, Josef was waiting for them. "Here," the bandit guide said to his friend, "a wedding gift." Remembering Gideon's dream, he presented him with a Kalashnikov of his own.

The guide had gathered fifty other travelers. Among them were a teenaged boy and his sister, a blind girl who would walk all the way to Sudan with a hand on her brother's shoulder.

Moving by night, sleeping by day, they retraced the route over the mountains, through the gorges, and across the wasteland. The August rains had been lighter than usual, but enough to fill the streams and water holes. The trip was going smoothly. "Too smoothly," Josef said with worry to Gideon.

For twelve days they avoided trouble. Close to Sudan, the weary caravan struggled up a steep hill. At the top of it, armed bandits were waiting.

"Your money!" the bandit leader demanded. Josef nodded grimly to Gideon. Outnumbered, they had to obey. A bandit passed among the frightened travelers, collecting whatever small sum each had.

"Not enough," the bandit leader growled. "Now we will take the young women."

The Kalashnikov hung on Gideon's shoulder, useless against guns already pointed and loaded. He let it slip to the ground. He approached the leader with the only weapon he had now—bluff.

"Maybe you should kill me first," he suggested, his voice level, his smile friendly. He stepped closer, offering his bare chest. "Then you can take the women."

The bandit stared, impassive. Gideon pointed a bony arm to where Esther stood. "Take them," Gideon offered again, still smiling. "But remember my name. I am Gideon of Woggera and that man is Josef of Armachiho."

The bandit shrugged.

"We have many friends," Gideon told him, "with many guns."

Gideon paused. The bandit had not yet blinked. "Take these women," Gideon told him, "but watch closely over your wives and your daughters." His voice was hard now, his smile gone. "Tomorrow, our friends will come for them. And the day after, they will come for you."

For a long moment, Gideon and the bandit stared at each other. Then the bandit turned away, and the caravan passed.

A day's walk from Sudan, Josef had to turn back. Gideon had still not fired the Kalashnikov, and he returned it to his friend.

"My brother, keep this for me," Gideon said. "One day, I think we will meet again."

Over the three hills, across the river that was muddy now but still passable, Gideon led the caravan into Sudan. That night, he and Esther lay awake in the stench of Um Rakuba. The next day, they rode the battered bus to Gedaref, where Gideon found a safe *tukul* for himself and his bride.

"Something is going to happen," he whispered to her. "Soon I will take you to a house in Jerusalem."

In other cities, other men were whispering, planning one final secret task for Gideon.

# Chapter 11

# *"The* Aliyah *Is Starting!"*

WITH HIS GO-AHEAD from the Geneva meeting, Jerry Weaver moved into high gear. Shuttling between Khartoum and Gedaref, he went shopping. This was not going to be the kind of operation where you could pull into a gas station and fill up at the pump. A big item on his list was fuel, lots of it—five hundred metric tons of it.

Fuel of any kind was scarce in Sudan, but Weaver knew the territory. Always a man to work slightly outside the system, he had the connections. He also had the money to outbid other buyers. He wasn't throwing it around and he was careful with his records, but over the next few weeks he would be spending a million dollars.

On the ground, it was Israeli money that paid the bills. Weaver would be spending great sums of money, with few questions asked. He would be buying unusual items in offbeat ways. Among his purchases was a pair of pearl-handled revolvers, bought to please a Sudanese official who yearned for this "gift."

In the Iran arms deal, American money may have paid for

112

a similar gift. In Sudan, according to Krieger, "we would not permit United States government money to be used that way." Instead, the Israelis passed some of the funds to Weaver in Geneva, and Israeli agents delivered other installments, as needed, in Sudan.

Weaver located the fuel through a broker from another Moslem country, and paid $175,000 for it. In fifty-five gallon drums, the fuel was delivered to an abandoned factory building that Weaver had rented in Gedaref. The place would also serve as an inconspicuous garage for the buses between trips to the airport.

Buses and cars were even harder to find than fuel in Sudan; the shortage of transportation was one of the reasons for the crisis in food and medicine at the camps. Weaver managed to find the five sturdy escort vehicles he figured he would need, but there were no buses for sale in the country.

With a carry-on suitcase crammed with cash, he flew to Saudi Arabia and bought four stripped-down truck frames. Shipped to Khartoum, they could be converted into buses. As the deadline edged closer, though, the work was still not finished. Weaver would have to peel off more bills and start the operation with rented buses.

There was still another transportation item. One of the key Sudanese officials—"*not* Nimeiry and *not* Tayeb"—had his eye on a small Piper airplane. It was sitting idle, left behind by an oil company that had shut down its operations. Weaver didn't need it for his own operation, but that made no difference. He bought the plane and, when the rescue was over, left it behind for a happy Sudanese officer.

Prowling the dusty streets of Gedaref, Weaver also hunted down blankets, food, and water. He stocked the buses with some of the supplies. He stored the rest in the American hideaway that would be their safe house in Gedaref. It sat on a quiet street on the edge of town, just a quick detour from the roads they would be traveling. It would be cramped, but in an emergency he could hide 200 to 250 Ethiopian Jews there for a night or two.

To keep emergencies to a minimum, the rescue team had to stay in constant communication. They needed radio receivers and transmitters. According to Mousa Ismail, an Amnul Dawla officer, Weaver gave him $150,000 for this communication equipment.

The Sudanese were busy, too. Traffic patterns and conditions at the Khartoum airport had to be checked and a landing strip cleared at its remote edge. A Sudan refugee official who asked too many questions was replaced with a state security officer. To cut down on rumors, the camps were closed to visitors.

Then personnel had to be assigned to guard the airport and escort the buses. For each trip there had to be at least one high-ranking officer, someone who would be obeyed without argument when he ordered the police at the checkpoints to "let them through."

The Sudan government would be paid for the use of its military and security personnel. The money came from Israel, but it was "laundered" by passing through American hands. The security department also would inherit the fleet of buses and cars that Weaver had put together.

How much baksheesh was there? In the past few years, Israeli agents had paid out millions of dollars to smooth the road out of Sudan. They were buying the winks and nods of high officials, the averted heads of rank-and-file soldiers and police, the forged travel passes and doctored exit visas they required.

Now, in Operation Moses, there were "gifts" for some of the high-ranking officers, but little if any baksheesh for the ordinary soldier. Sudanese guarded the convoys, manned the checkpoints, drove the buses, refueled the planes. Most of them were told they were transporting "ordinary refugees," poor, tattered people who were being legally resettled in other countries. "If you're moving refugees around in Sudan," Weaver asked, "who cares?" If some of the Sudanese suspected they were helping to smuggle Jews, they still had their orders to follow, orders that came from the president and vice-president.

The operation was falling into place, but slower than its planners had hoped. The first target date was the end of October. It edged into early November, but the logistics were still not in place. Instead, in early November, Americans, Israelis, and refugee officials met once again in Geneva to set a final date, the third week of November.

Meanwhile, Senator Edward Kennedy was heading their way, with news reporters and TV cameras in his wake. Concerned about the famine, Kennedy was touring the scene. His agenda called for Christmas in Gedaref, when Operation Moses might still be running. If someone in his entourage sniffed out the secret, that would be it. At almost the last moment, Kennedy changed his plans. He would be visiting Kassala and the refugee camps around that city. It was far enough north to keep his entourage from stumbling over the operation.

The Israelis, too, had gone shopping. They found the planes they needed in Brussels, Belgium, through a charter company known as Trans European Airways. Its president, George Gutelman, a middle-aged Jew, had done business with Israel before. As a Jerusalem official noted, he was "well known to many of us" and could be counted on to be discreet. Like the Sudanese, the Belgian was not told that it was American money paying for the planes.

Gutelman also had connections with Sudan. No one would be surprised to see TEA planes land in Khartoum; they came there regularly to pick up Moslem pilgrims on the way to Mecca. This was a charter to a different holy city, but Gutelman knew how to choose flight crews who were tight-lipped and disciplined. For this operation, he found a quiet hotel for them, away from the bustle and temptation of downtown Khartoum.

Before flying on to Israel, thousands of Jewish refugees would have to touch down in "a third country," as they called it. So Israel was also in the market for friendly stopovers.

Brussels was ideal. If the planes left from there, it was simpler and tidier for them to return to home base. They would attract less attention there.

Again Gutelman was helpful. He had friends in high places, including the key man in Belgium they needed on their side, Jean Gol, then the government minister who was responsible for the Belgian security service. Through Gol, with Israel's promise of secrecy, they won the agreement of the prime minister.

In one or two other countries, other governments agreed that their airports could be used. Security counted. Everywhere it was on a need-to-know basis. By one account, even the Ministry of Foreign Affairs in Belgium was not informed. The Europeans were nervous about leaks that might hurt their relations with sensitive Arab nations. No one wanted rumors that would provoke the wrath of Arab terrorists.

Within the borders of Israel, there were other cautious preparations. Yehuda Dominitz and other Jewish Agency officials alerted a few of their key immigration specialists. "One day," they were told, "we are going to bring the Ethiopian Jews here, to Israel. Sooner or later, whenever it happens, you must be ready for them." Quietly, space was set aside in the existing absorption centers, halfway houses for new immigrants, and new centers were readied. Arrangements were made for social workers, medical teams, translators, and other helping hands.

Meanwhile, one or two Ethiopian Jews were smuggled in reverse—from Israel to Sudan. Though most of the Jews were crowded into the Tawawa and Um Rakuba refugee camps, the ones close to Gedaref, others were scattered in more distant camps. Now the list makers like Gideon would have to find them, identify them, and prepare them for the *aliyah*.

Everything was now in place. On the American side, Ambassador Horan passed the message to Washington. The word came back: "Go!"

Just six weeks after the secret meetings in Geneva, on November 20, 1984, the first caravan of buses would leave Gedaref and race for the plane in Khartoum.

"When will we go to Jerusalem?" little Tzion asked.

"Maybe next week," Malka Alemie answered at first.

"Maybe next month," she said later.

After a while, the child stopped asking. In Um Rakuba, in that terrible spring and summer of 1984, they no longer knew what day or month it was. For Malka, hope was the next sunrise. "Let us all be alive tomorrow," she prayed.

On a pallet of straw, her son, Eigal, lay trembling and delirious with malaria. He shivered with cold one minute and fever the next. Malka tightened the blanket around him and brushed the flies from his face. "Are his eyes less yellow today?" she hoped. "Is he any better?"

In her arms, her daughter-in-law, Kohava, held the baby she had carried out of Ethiopia in an *ankelba.* For three days the baby had been shaking. His head burned with fever. He was too weak to suckle at his mother's breast, too weak even to whimper.

"Dysentery," the Sudanese doctor had said, giving her a handful of tetracycline capsules for the baby. Yesterday she had given him the medicine; today he seemed worse.

"The medicine is bad," Kohava insisted, her eyes wild with fear. Um Rakuba, "Mother of Shelter" in Arabic, was a place of death—and paranoia. Crowded together in *tukuls* built on the swampy ground of an old cemetery, still falashas, still strangers in an enemy land, the Ethiopian Jews told each other stories.

People said there was poison in the injections that the doctors gave the little children. They suspected the capsules of medicine, too. As a test, some people heated them on the fire and pointed to the bad smell as proof. Others said there were bits of ground glass and razor blades mixed in with the healing grains of medicine.

"I want to see what's in the medicine," Kohava insisted. As Malka emptied the capsule onto a dish, the young mother studied the small grains of medicine. "There!" she shouted. "There's something shiny."

Kohava was certain she had seen a fatal glint. Before Malka could see it too, the young mother threw the dish of medicine to the ground.

The next day, the baby stopped shaking. At ten months old, he was dead. Kohava's premonition had come true. She remembered the discarded *ankelba* that another grieving mother had left on the trail out of Ethiopia. "Now I will throw away the *ankelba,* too," she wept.

Had the baby died because of the medicine they gave it, or the medicine they tossed away? Was the child too sick for any medicine to help? Malka had no answers. At Kohava's insistence, she threw away her handful of malaria pills and prayed that her son, Eigal, would get better without them.

The truth was as terrible as the stories the falashas told each other. When the Alemies arrived, there was no well or other water supply in the falasha section of Um Rakuba. Instead, water was brought in large oil drums, hauled on donkeys from the freshwater taps of the Amharic part of the camp. The metal drums, never quite clean, were a breeding place for microbes. Each day, as the falashas filled their canteens with this water, they were pouring out disease.

The UNHCR had a subsistence level for the refugee camps, an amount of nutrition that would keep people barely alive. The daily ration was supposed to be a pound of flour for each person, along with a tablespoon each of peas, oil, and dried milk. Yet for most of the spring and summer of 1984, the refugees were getting only half that meager ration.

Everyone was hungry, but the falashas were closer to starvation than anyone else. There were special feeding stations for young children, but many of the Jews were afraid to go there.

At one point, the daily allotment of oil was Norwegian whale fat. It was not kosher, forbidden by their dietary laws, and many of the falashas refused to use it. On the rare days when there was a bit of meat, they refused that, too, as not kosher. "If we are going to die," they decided stubbornly, "let it be as Jews."

"We are so few," Malka grieved, "and so many are dying." She despaired for little Tzion, who had turned four years old, and his sister Orit, who is six now. The two children sat in the dirt in front of the *tukul,* too weak and too frightened to play.

They felt surrounded by enemies, beset from all sides. If a man wandered down the wrong path, he might be beaten. If a woman went for water, she might be insulted. Some had been raped.

There was nowhere to hide from dysentery and dehydration, typhus and measles, malaria and malnutrition. Weakened by their trek, the falashas were vulnerable to the strange diseases of a different land and to its terrible, sometimes blinding infections. Coming from the cool highlands of Ethiopia, they felt life ebbing away in the Sudan heat.

With nowhere to go, some of the other Ethiopian refugees settled in, built sturdier houses, hired themselves out as workers on nearby farms, and set up shops and even brothels. The falashas cowered in tents and straw huts. They were afraid to work with metal or pottery, lest their skills give them away as Jews. They had expected to be whisked away to Israel, yet month after month they lingered here.

Malka remembered the story of the first exodus out of Egypt. Hungry, thirsty, exhausted, the Jews had despaired. "Did you bring us away to die in the wilderness," they asked Moses, "because there were no graves in Egypt?"

There were graves enough in Sudan. It is estimated that from two to four thousand Ethiopian Jews died there, and many people think the high guess is the more accurate one. A British professor, Tudor Parfitt, counted the graves and managed to see the camp's own records. Just in Um Rakuba, just in the months from April to November 1984, according to the ledgers, 1,939 falashas died, and 1,202 of them were children under the age of fifteen.

The falashas hid their sick and stood guard over their dying. They were afraid the camp guards would not let them be buried according to Jewish custom. With so much death, they suspected that the guards would take the bodies and throw them into a mass ditch.

On a single day, Malka counted twenty bodies being carried to the falasha cemetery at Um Rakuba. One day it was the old *kes* who had led their prayers on the trek. The mourners were weak with hunger and disease, and sometimes it took half a dozen of them to carry one wasted body. Dry-eyed, beyond tears, they dug a shallow grave, then covered it with a cairn of stones. When she could, Malka helped. "Tomorrow I may be the one who's dead," she explained, "and I'll need someone to carry me to the grave."

With all her strength, Malka tried to focus on life. Each day she picked up their meager rations. The sorghum flour was black and smelled of decay. Her fingers sifted through it, picking out the dead bugs and bits of dirt, feeling for something else as well. She never found any, but people said there was ground glass and razor blades in the flour, too.

Desperate, she asked another refugee, a Christian who spoke English, to explain their fears to the UNHCR representative. Something was lost in the translation. The white man gave her a sympathetic smile, but nothing changed.

"The children will die with this food," Malka anguished. Once again, she made up her mind. She would find a way to speak to the UNHCR representative herself. Without words, acting out her message, she showed him a bowl of flour. Then she picked some up in her fingers and pretended to eat it. In a pantomime of agony, she clutched her stomach and fell to the ground.

Now they understood. In late September, good white flour began to arrive from the United States and Canada, but it did not always reach the refugees. Some of the workers in the camp sold it for a profit and instead distributed spoiled sorghum flour, laced with worms and bugs. Finally, an angry American—"a woman doctor," Malka marveled—put a stop to it. She stood on the food lines with Malka and the other refugees, making certain that they received the nourishing flour that had been sent for them.

They were putting bandages on the gaping sores of Um Rakuba. All along there had been drilling equipment in the area, to dig the water well that was missing from the falasha section of the camp and also to dig additional wells that were needed by the Christian and Moslem refugees. "But there were disputes over turf among the different United Nations agencies," Krieger explained, "and the people who had the drills wouldn't make them available." Finally, the Americans had to turn to an oil company with a spare drilling rig, borrowing it to dig the lifesaving water wells.

At the clinic, there was less fear and suspicion now. Little Tzion and then Orit grew hot with fever. "Like the baby," Kohava worried. She allowed the new doctors to give them an injection. She fed them the new capsules she'd been given and watched them grow stronger. When Eigal had a second attack of malaria, she gave him the new quinine pills. "We can trust the American medicine," she told everyone.

For Malka, the nightmare continued. On the trek, she'd thought she heard gunshots in the distance. In Sudan, she asked every new arrival about her family. "Have you seen my husband?" she asked. "And my daughters?"

Finally, someone had an answer for her. Government troops had surrounded the caravan and fired on them. Outnumbered, the guides had abandoned the Jews and fled. The people were arrested, held for a time, and then scattered, no one knew where.

Malka sighed. When they left Ethiopia, the sun still rose in the east, in Gondar province, and set in Metamma, on the Sudan border, an evil place in falasha legend. They had crossed the border to the far side of that sunset. "Now the sun rises in Metamma," she wept. "The world is turned upside down."

It was the end of November, and the sun hung in the Sudan sky, pitiless and blazing. Malka made her way past the crowded *tukuls* and through the narrow passageways, streets that had become open sewers. She no longer noticed the reek of human waste and the stench of death. As she did every day, she was going to pick up the flour ration.

As she waited her turn, she listened to the voices around her. There were always rumors, complaints, reports of a sick child, but today there was something different.

"Those poor falashas," a man was saying. "They are pushing them out of Tawawa."

"They are dying in that camp and they will die in another," his friend answered. "Why do they force them to make such a trip?"

If they were moving the Jews of Tawawa, Malka understood why. She wanted to race back to her family, but she forced herself to walk calmly. Tears were running down her gaunt cheeks, but she was laughing, too. Excited, exultant, she gathered her family around her.

"The *aliyah*," she told them. "It's starting." They stared at her. "Yes, yes, the *aliyah*." She hugged little Tzion to her. "Soon, very soon, we are going to Jerusalem."

From *tukul* to wretched *tukul*, the word spread. Is it true at last? they wondered. They heard one piece of information, then another. Four buses had come to take people from Tawawa to another place. "Where?" Malka asked. No one knew its name, but from this other place they would go to Jerusalem.

When Gideon appeared the next day, they crowded around

him. "Stay here and say nothing," the bony young messenger told them. "When we have taken the people out of Tawawa, we will come for you."

Gideon guessed what they were thinking. "Don't come to Tawawa," he urged. "Be patient awhile longer."

But the Alemie family had waited in the purgatory called Um Rakuba for seven months, and they could wait no more. "What if something happens?" Malka worried. "What if the *aliyah* stops and we are left behind?"

At night, pooling their meager funds with forty other people, they hired a truck driver to take them the fifty miles from Um Rakuba to Tawawa. In the Jewish section of that camp there were newly empty huts, and the Alemies moved into one of them.

"Look," Malka said. In front of the hut, a last ember still glowed in the cooking fire. Her voice trembled and her hands fluttered. "This very night, these people have gone to Jerusalem."

# Chapter 12

# "On the Wings of Eagles"

OPERATION MOSES BEGAN in confusion. On November 20, 1984, as the sun was setting, the four rented buses lumbered across an open field. Battered hulks, with empty openings for windows, they parked at the edge of the Tawawa refugee camp. It was the only part of that night's rescue that took place exactly as planned.

Sudan security officers moved out to protect the scene. Jerry Weaver watched anxiously as an Ethiopian Jew, the son of a famous falasha family, was swallowed up by the shadows of the camp.

Just the day before, he'd been slipped into Sudan, sent by the Israelis to gather and lead the Jews out of the camps. Quiet and gentle, he seemed frail to Weaver. He spoke in the typical murmur of Ethiopia, a soft voice, hard for Western ears to make out, and he made Weaver nervous.

A half-hour passed and no one emerged from the camps. Weaver checked his watch. He didn't want to be late getting to the airport.

Inside the camp, the quiet Ethiopian was stronger than

Weaver thought. He had led men into battle in the 1973 war, but today he faced an impossible task. He was supposed to send out the most vulnerable people first, the children, the sick, and the elderly. Clutching at him, clamoring to be saved, everyone wanted to be first.

Wretched scarecrows crowded around the man, and then pushed past him. Once, in Ethiopia, they'd had a quiet dignity. In the misery and fear of Sudan, they had waited patiently. Now they became a mob, stampeded by hope.

Ten people emerged from the camp. Then twenty. Then hundreds of people were running toward the buses, men and women, mothers with babies and old men with canes.

The quiet Ethiopian struggled to reach the door of the first bus, to check off the passengers on his list, but they surged past him. The Ethiopian tried to push them back. Desperate, some were trying to crawl through the windows; others were climbing onto the bus roof. Weaver grabbed a cane and tried to beat them back. Nothing could stop them. Shoving and shouting, they forced their way onto the buses.

"Let's go!" Weaver ordered. It had taken an hour and a half just to load the buses. Finally, with no idea of how many refugees they were carrying, the convoy moved out.

In the pandemonium, with people still racing after the buses, they took a wrong turn and found themselves on a dirt road. "Damn!" Weaver swore. "It's easy to get confused in this country." With a grinding of gears, all four buses and the five escort vehicles had to turn around and retrace the route to the Gedaref-Khartoum road.

After only a few minutes, they were stopped by a pair of traffic policemen. The headlight of one of the buses was out, a violation. The ranking Sudanese officer hurried from his car at the rear of the convoy. After some discussion, and a look at the officer's identification card, the traffic policemen waved the convoy on.

With a five-hour drive to make with a load of mysterious

passengers, the drivers were nervous. They pressed harder and harder, faster and faster. Weaver rode with the Sudanese officers, bringing up the rear, watching for trouble. Their car was racing along at seventy-five miles per hour, but all they could see of the buses was their dust.

Weaver swore again. He caught up with the buses at the first checkpoint. "Take it easy," he ordered the drivers. "Keep it down to seventy."

At each police checkpoint, there was a halt for questions and arguments. "Who are these people?" the officers demanded, pointing at the frightened faces in the bus windows. "Ordinary refugees," came the answer. If there was more debate, something was muttered about "resettlement programs," rank was pulled, and the convoy was allowed to pass.

About ten miles from Khartoum, other Sudanese security officers were waiting for them at the checkpoint—with bad news. "You'll have to stop here," they were told.

Weaver groaned. He'd thought the plane from Brussels, a Boeing 707, would be waiting for them at the airport, refueled and ready for takeoff. Now he heard that it hadn't even landed yet.

The convoy pulled off and waited at the side of the road. Weaver was edgy. If too much time passed, they might have to take the people to the safe house and keep them there overnight. After the near riot at Tawawa, the buses, loaded now with 283 people, were strangely quiet. The only sound was a baby's cry, stifled quickly by the mother.

An hour ticked by. In the dark night, they strained to hear the sound of an airplane engine. Finally, a Sudanese messenger drove up, with word that the plane had landed. It was refueled and serviced. The Frenchman who watched every move, missing nothing, was an Israeli agent.

The convoy drove the last few miles to the rear gate of the airport. The buses lumbered across the tarmac and came to a

A falasha family in the Um Rakuba refugee camp, 1984. The camp was established in 1976 for two thousand refugees, and by November 1984 there were more than twenty thousand Jews, Christians, and Moslems huddled there. *(Photo by Tudor Parfitt.)*

Malka Alemie in her Sabbath
*mise,* the traditional Ethiop
dress. The cloth was woven by
husband, the decoration emb.
dered by herself. On the long t
out of her village, Malka carr
this dress with her. Today
wears it to attend a synagogu
Israel. *(Photo by John Milton I*
*liams.)*

Tzion Alemie, happy to be in the promised land.
*(Photo by John Milton Williams.)*

Ethiopian children making menorahs for their first Hanukkah in Israel. Their ancestors had left Jerusalem before the events that this holiday celebrates. *(Photo by John Milton Williams.)*

This *kes* arrived in Israel carrying "the things of Moses," the Torah that his people had as a handwritten book rather than the traditional Jewish scroll. *(Photo by UJA Press Service.)*

Israeli Prime Minister Shimon Peres with one of his newest citizens. Just hours after they arrived in Israel, the Ethiopians no longer recognized themselves. They had stripped away the tattered clothes of Africa and changed into modern dress. *(Photo by UJA Press Service.)*

Training on a paramilitary course in Israel during 1984. *(Photo by Doron Bacher. Courtesy of Beth Hatefutsoth, The Nahum Goldmann Museum of the Jewish Diaspora.)*

The Chief Rabbis of Israel required that Beta Israel undergo special ritual immersion before marriage. In protest against the ruling, fifteen couples held a group wedding in April 1986, according to the Ethiopian tradition. *(Photo by Doron Bacher. Courtesy of Beth Hatefutsoth, The Nahum Goldmann Museum of the Jewish Diaspora.)*

Celebration of the Beta Israel holiday Seged in Jerusalem. *(Photos by Doron Bacher. Courtesy of Beth Hatefutsoth, The Nahum Goldmann Museum of the Jewish Diaspora.)*

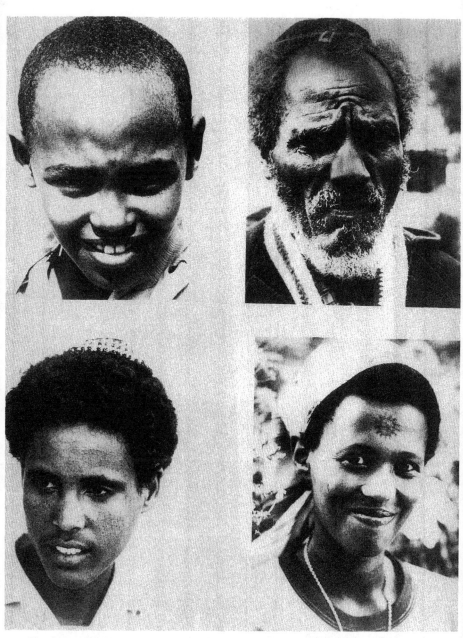

The faces of Ethiopia. *(Photos by UJA Press Service.)*

A Beta Israel woman with neck tattoos. "The tattoos ward off the goiter," she explains. Later, with a shy smile, she admits, "It's stylish in Ethiopia. It's a sign of beauty." *(Photo by John Milton Williams.)*

"But where is the rest of my family?" An elderly woman remembers the trek out of Ethiopia and the people who are still trapped there. *(Photo by John Milton Williams.)*

stop at the airplane steps. The first dazed and tattered refugees climbed aboard. Some were so weak they had to be carried.

Then the Belgian pilot balked. Children were jammed two or three together in some of the seats of his plane. There were more people than there were oxygen masks. There were dozens more than the normal load of 220 passengers.

The pilot was refusing to take off with such violations. The Israeli agent confronted him, and there was a loud argument in French. The agent wanted no more problems and no more delays. If the pilot didn't want to fly, they would find somebody else who was willing. Still fuming, the pilot took his seat in the cockpit.

Finally, in the early hours of November 21, the first plane rose into the air.

The Sudanese were furious. If there were pandemonium like this again, the whole world would know what they were up to. They were threatening to call off the operation.

Two nights later, they tried again. Inside the camp, Gideon and the other list makers worked with the quiet Ethiopian, trying to organize the exodus. "How can we choose?" Gideon asked. "Am I God? Are you? How can we say 'You stay' and 'You go'?"

Yet they had to choose. Many of the refugees remembered the quiet man's father. He was their past and their future, and some touched him shyly, as if the dust of the promised land might still cling to him. Others offered money for a chance to go there sooner. Parents pushed their children forward. "Take my son today," a mother begged. "Tomorrow, he could be dead in this place."

Gideon understood. His wife, Esther, was still hiding in a *tukul* in Gedaref, and he would have given almost anything to bring her here and put her on one of those first buses. He sighed. If he put his wife ahead of those other people, it would dishonor both of them.

"Please sit down. Please wait," the man pleaded with the desperate crowd. "We will come back for you tomorrow."

Still, people pushed past him, a wave of misery pouring out of the camp. For each bus, with room for fifty or sixty people, there were two hundred trying to clamber on. There was still too much confusion and too much dangerous noise, but it went smoother than the first trip. There were no wrong turns. They arrived in Khartoum close to schedule, and the plane was waiting.

The Sudanese agreed to continue, on an every-other-night schedule. Weaver and a Sudanese aide took turns organizing each convoy. Weaver was going full speed, twenty hours a day, living on adrenaline. Along with the exodus, he was doing business-as-usual at the embassy. For appearance's sake, to avoid any questions, he was still looking after normal refugee affairs and shepherding senators and other VIP visitors.

There were still glitches, moments that called for cool heads and fast action. A bus broke down and had to be replaced quickly with a truck. At the airport, a Bulgarian, an employee with one of the airlines, sniffed too close to the secret and was hustled out of the country. At the airplane steps, a father panicked, refused to climb into the belly of "this big bird," and ran screaming into the night. His son, age ten, living now in an Israeli youth village, still waits for word of him.

Inside the camp, the quiet Ethiopian and the list makers struggled for a semblance of order. It came slowly. "The children," people cried out. "Take the children." Of all the hard choices, this was the easiest. One trip was made up of almost all children, with only enough adults to look after the littlest ones. Half of the people flown to Israel were young children.

As people saw the buses coming back again and again, they began to trust in tomorrow. Now Gideon brought Esther to Tawawa and placed her on one of the buses. She was in the first weeks of pregnancy and, whatever else happened, they wanted the baby to be born in Israel. "Think of it," Gideon whispered.

"After all the generations, a child of our family will be born in the promised land."

When the airlift began, no one knew exactly how many Ethiopian Jews were in Tawawa. About two thousand, they guessed. Yet when fifteen hundred had been flown out, the *tukuls* were more crowded than ever. From Um Rakuba and other camps, families like the Alemies were arriving on their own.

The refugee team shrugged and kept going. These people were an enigma. They listened to voices that other people did not hear. Driven by prophecy, they moved to their own secret signals.

Gideon understood. Moving among the newcomers to Tawawa, he welcomed Malka. In another *tukul,* he embraced his father, a new arrival on one of Josef's caravans. The grandfather, the old storyteller, had died, but Gideon's father pointed to someone else. "Look who's here with me," he said and laughed. A great-aunt, a woman of ninety, had hobbled on her cane across the mountains and desert to reach this place. Elsewhere, Gideon recognized a husband and wife from Gondar, Christian schoolteachers who had led their young Jewish students out of Ethiopia and watched over them during the long months in Sudan.

After a while, the operation was going smoothly enough to shift to a daily schedule of flights. The safe house in Gedaref stayed quiet and empty, unused except as an occasional crash pad for Weaver's trips from Khartoum. They had two bus crews now, one on the road, one sleeping between trips at the Amnul Dawla's safe house in Khartoum.

Now Gideon and the quiet Ethiopian came to Tawawa by day, to organize each night's exodus. "Be ready tonight," they told some people. "Your turn is tomorrow," they promised others. "Be patient a little longer," they pleaded with the rest.

Parents still pushed their children forward into the arms of strangers. Few families left as a complete unit, all on the same trip. But Malka Alemie held her own family back. "Wait, wait," she told them. "We must not be separated. We must arrive in Jerusalem together."

Late one afternoon, Gideon found her. "Gather up your family," he whispered. "When the sun goes down, we will take you on the bus."

"At last." Malka smiled. Her heart pounded with excitement and then fear. As she looked around, she realized her family was scattered. Her son, Eigal, had gone to the town with a few coins to buy some food. Little Tzion was nowhere to be seen. Was he with her teenaged daughter, fetching water, or had he wandered away by himself? Malka's hands fluttered and flew to her throat. After seven months in Um Rakuba and three weeks in Tawawa, would they be separated now?

"Don't move," Malka told the family members who were there in the *tukul.* She paced in front of the hut, a few steps down one path and then another. Here, thank heaven, was Tzion. There, carrying the jug of water, was her daughter. "Hurry," she beckoned. The sky was darkening when Eigal finally returned.

"Quickly, this way," Gideon told them, and the Alemies hurried toward the waiting bus. "Alemie," the list maker called out at the door of the bus, counting off the family members as they entered.

An excited Tzion peered through the bus window. "Look at those guns!" For secrecy's sake, the Sudanese security officers were in mufti; they had left their uniforms but not their weapons at home. Malka marveled at the unlikely allies who were guarding a falasha convoy. Still, at each checkpoint she tensed, holding her breath until the buses started up again.

For five hours the buses jounced and rattled along the road to Khartoum. Then they were there, parked in the airport darkness, staring at shadows. "Hurry," someone said, and strange hands propelled them forward.

"*If I take wings like an eagle,*" an old falasha psalm promised, *"and fly to the ends of the sea, there Thy hand guides me and Thy right hand places me."*

The Alemies were among the first to climb down from the bus. Malka walked a few steps across the tarmac and then started up the longest flight of stairs she had ever seen. At the top, she found herself in an amazing place. She was escorted to a big chair, softer than any she'd ever known.

"Such a nice house," she marveled. Then the "house" began to move, the noise of its takeoff startling her. A medical team moved up and down the aisle, rebandaging old wounds, hooking up intravenous bottles for some of the feeble passengers, starting the healing process in midair. A young woman in a uniform offered coffee and a pillow for Malka's weary head.

She leaned back. Tears slid down her hollow cheeks. She was flying to Jerusalem, but where was her husband, Rachamim? Where were her daughters?

"Grandma?" Little Tzion pulled worriedly at her sleeve. She tried to smile at him. Her hands flew to dab at her eyes, but the tears kept coming. Finally, she was safe enough to cry.

Hours later, the plane touched down smoothly. She stared out the window. "This is Europe," someone told her. A short while later, they were in the air again.

The sun was rising as they landed in Israel. As they walked from the plane, many of the people knelt to kiss the ground. Malka knelt too.

"Come," she told little Tzion. "Taste the land of Israel." Smiling, she asked, "Is it not sweet?"

Some of the passengers had to be carried off in stretchers. Ambulances were waiting, and about one in five was taken directly from the airport to a hospital. To the Israelis, there was something terribly familiar about these new arrivals. Their clothes were different, and their skin darker, but they had the same skeletal bodies and dazed, haunted looks that had been seen forty years earlier, on concentration-camp survivors.

At the edge of the tarmac, a crowd of people had waited for hours to welcome the plane. Some of them were crying at the sight of a lost tribe coming home again.

So many white people, Malka thought. She looked around in amazement. Can they all be Jews?

# Chapter 13

# The Eagle Falters

OPERATION MOSES MOVED along smoothly, but new refugees were arriving every day from Ethiopia. Gideon met a group of them at the Sudan border one evening, planning to lead them straight to the Tawawa camp. Then, from the shadows, someone called out the list maker's Moslem name.

"Hassan!"

Gideon turned, startled. Suddenly, he was face to face with his Sudanese captain.

"Who are these people?" the captain demanded. "What are you doing with them?"

"They are poor Christians from Ethiopia," Gideon lied. He watched the captain's face, hoping to be believed one last time. "I was telling them that the Moslems of Sudan will be kind to them."

"Wait here," the captain commanded. He walked a few paces and spoke rapidly to two soldiers, as if issuing orders. Gideon tensed, wondering if he was about to be arrested.

Instead, when the captain walked back, he was smiling. "It's all arranged," he said. He led Gideon and the falasha refugees to a *tukul* where they could rest overnight. At dawn, he ordered a truck to take them to Tawawa.

"I hear there are empty *tukuls* there," he said. The captain looked dapper as usual, but tired. "Is your mother still crying?" he asked with a small, ironic smile.

"No," Gideon whispered. "Not anymore."

The captain studied the young man's face, as if trying to come to a decision. "Did you ever guess?" Gideon wanted to ask. "I am sorry for the lies," he wanted to say. Instead, silently, he held out a hand, trembling slightly, to his old friend. With his other hand, he touched the forearm of the extended one, an Ethiopian gesture of respect. The captain stared. With a sigh, he took the hand in his.

"*As-salaam alekum,*" the captain said in Arabic. "Peace be with you." Then he turned on his heels.

"*Alekum as-salaam,*" Gideon called after him. "With you be peace."

Yet peace is elusive in this part of the world, and very soon mothers would be crying again. In Tawawa, Gideon went about his job, not knowing that Operation Moses was about to crash.

When the planes flew the first falashas to freedom, the operation was nameless and its planners were anonymous. It was urgent to keep it that way. Only a few Mossad agents had a code name for it: *Gur Aryeh Yehudah,* the Lion of Judah's Cub.

Then a secret meeting was held in New York City between Israeli officials and leaders of the United Jewish Appeal (UJA), the fund-raising arm of American Jewry.

The Israelis announced a miracle in the making, the return of a lost tribe. "Whether we can afford it or not, whether we have the money or not," they said, "we are bringing these people out."

They hoped that the Jews of the world would help with a part of the cost. Human lives can't be counted in dollars, but the bill for this immigration and resettlement would eventually soar past the $300 million mark, a staggering amount for a country in economic crisis.

For now, the Israelis had set a target of $82 million from the people of the diaspora, with $60 million of that to come from American Jews. As they agreed, it would be easier to raise those funds during the drama of the rescue. As they warned, the fund raising would have to be almost as secret as the airlift itself.

A few days later, the UJA leaders met in a brainstorming session. They were looking for ways and means, slogans and catchwords. "Operation Moses," someone called out. It was a perfect name for the fund-raising campaign. Very quickly, it also became the name of the secret exodus.

Across the United States, in cities and suburbs, there were small gatherings in private homes and larger meetings in synagogues. One slogan urged, "Give $6,000 to save a life." It was more of a catchy phrase than an actual, lifesaving figure, but some big donors gave that and much more. Others gave what they could, ten- and twenty-dollar donations that added up to reach the goal.

In one city, afraid that they didn't have enough money to give, a congregation offered to mortgage its synagogue. Everywhere, remembering the Holocaust, American Jews told each other, "If only we could have done this in Germany." In the drama of the moment, they celebrated, agreeing, "This is what Israel was created for."

The UJA campaign tried to be discreet, with no fanfare or printed materials. It talked of rescuing Ethiopian Jews who were trapped in the refugee camps of "an African country"; Sudan was never mentioned. It was a triumph; the campaign reached across the country, into almost every synagogue and Jewish organization. No other campaign, no other charity or group of charities, had ever raised so much money so quickly. Yet as they talked to so many people, as they raised the $60 million, they also raised some awkward questions.

Inevitably, the story leaked out. Early in December, the *New*

*York Times* was preparing an article on Operation Moses. Alerted about this, Naftali Lavi, Consul General of Israel in New York City, placed an emergency phone call to Van Nuys, California. He asked Phil Blazer, publisher of *Israel Today,* to telephone his newspaper friends. When Blazer explained how "sensitive" the story was, the *Times'* foreign editor, Warren Hoge, agreed to spike it.

Lives were at stake, but a week later the story appeared in two Jewish-American weeklies. With that, the *Times* and other papers felt that they, too, had to publish. They kept the first report terse and short on details. If the Sudanese read it, there was no reaction. The story was allowed to fade.

Then a more fatal leak sprang, this time in Israel. A small West Bank newsletter, *Nequeda,* published the story on January 3, 1986. Other Israeli papers, thinking that the news blackout was lifted, rushed to publish it too.

The world press had been holding back on the story. Now that it had broken in Israel, they clamored for more information. The next day, on orders from Prime Minister Shimon Peres, there was a government press conference.

With that, the airlift crashed. A newspaper story here and there was one thing; Sudan could ignore it, even deny it. An official statement by the Israeli government was something else.

Two more planes managed to leave Khartoum. Then, on January 6, Sudan canceled the operation.

The Ethiopian Jews who had managed to reach Israel were distraught. What now? What would happen to the parents, the brothers and sisters still trapped in Africa? In the Old City of Jerusalem, a group of Ethiopian children stood barefoot at the Western Wall, touching the remnant of the old Temple with trembling hands, praying for the remnant of their people.

Peres may have thought he could limit the stories that came out of the press conference. The plan was to tell the world about how Israel was welcoming and caring for her new citizens, and to avoid questions about the secret ways they had arrived in the country. Yet those were the details the reporters were clamoring for, and there was no controlling the damage.

In Jerusalem, an Israeli official, a man who'd been at those secret Geneva meetings, accused Peres of playing politics. "A banking scandal was making big news," he charged. "To get that off the front pages, Peres called the press conference about Operation Moses." With a wry smile, he asked, "How else can you explain it? Maybe it was just plain stupid, but I'm not going to think that about the Israeli government."

In Washington, they were "stunned." There was "significant irritation," as they put it, at the State Department; the Americans felt they'd gone out on a limb, only to have Israel saw it off.

Mournfully, they held a post-mortem about a secret operation that was now front-page news. "Sudan had to cancel it," one official said. "Once the news was out, what else could a member of the Arab League do?"

Until the Israeli press conference, the operation had gone more smoothly than they had dared to hope. How many people were stranded now in the Sudanese camps? They guessed—wrongly, as it turned out—about twelve hundred.

"Damn, we were so close," Richard Krieger exploded. "Just a few more days and we could have pulled it off. We could have saved them all."

In Tawawa, Gideon did not understand what had happened. On the Saturday night of January 5, he knew only that the *aliyah* was halted. He was here to gather people for the last convoy.

"Go quickly," he told one family, hurrying them in the direction of the waiting buses.

"Wait a little longer," he told another family. "We will come back for you."

It was the hardest lie he had ever told. He suspected that it would be a long wait for these trapped people. Quickly, he turned away, his eyes shining with tears.

Over the next weeks, he had a more terrible job. Hundreds of falashas were on the road, making their way out of the villages and toward Sudan. Gideon and other messengers slipped across the Atbara River to meet them on the Ethiopian side of the border.

The travelers were exhausted. Whatever food and water they'd had was now gone. Some were near death. "The *aliyah* has stopped," Gideon had to tell them. "You must turn back."

Operation Moses lasted for forty-seven days. They made thirty-six flights and rescued seventy-eight hundred people. When the secret operation ended in that January dawn, it made headlines around the world.

In the United States, the press had bravos for Israel. "For the first time in history," the *New York Times* announced, "thousands of black people are being brought into a country not in chains but as citizens."

In England there were cheers. "There are no lengths to which Israel will not go to protect its people, as in the raid on Entebbe, or to avenge them, as in the capture of Eichmann," said an editorial in the *Guardian.* "No other country would have had the nerve to grab many thousands of people from the mountains of East Africa and fly them to another continent. . . . As a famine relief operation, nothing could be more convincing than to gather up the victims and take them where there is plenty of food."

In Africa, where Israel had made and then lost so many friends, there was some polite applause. As the *Weekly Review* of Nairobi, Kenya, said, " . . . the fact that Falashas are Africans cannot be ignored, even by anti-Israel critics who have in the past equated Zionism with racism."

The men at the State Department read the papers nervously. They were relieved to find that the international spotlight had focused on the Israelis.

If the Western world hailed the airlift, the Eastern world

denounced it. In the Soviet Union it was attacked as a plot "to colonize occupied Arab territories." The Soviet-bloc media saw the falashas as potential Israeli soldiers, and so did most of the Arab world.

Ethiopia blamed both Sudan and Israel. Her leaders complained that the falashas were not really Jews but Ethiopian citizens who had been "abducted." In an interview with the Canadian Broadcasting Company, Colonel Mengistu expressed his fury: "These people were forced from our territory, from parts of Ethiopia where we do not have very tight security. They were almost dragged against their will to go to Israel. This act is illegal and inhuman, and indeed it is an indirect form of slavery."

In Khartoum, the walls were plastered with posters that accused Nimeiry of "collaboration with the Zionist enemy." Around the Arab world there was the same denunciation. In self-defense, a Sudanese official protested that "every Arab government has clandestine links with Israel."

According to a Saudi Arabian daily paper, *Sharak al-Awasat*, published in London, "The airlift . . . hurt the Arab man-in-the-street and raised his blood pressure." Yet the Saudi paper also raised an unexpected question:

What is the source of the Israeli's interest in this community of Falashan Jews? It emanates from the importance the Jew attaches to his Jewish brother—ideologically and nationally.

A Jew, even in Eskimoland [sic], is always a Jew, and it is incumbent upon "the state of his destination" to take an interest in him and to take care of him until he returns to what is called the Land of the Bible, where he will enjoy its protection.

The issue of the intrinsic worth of the human being, or his humanity—that is the source of their strength . . . and the source of our weakness.

# Chapter 14

# Operation Sheba

BUSTLING, IMPATIENT, CONTRADICTORY, Israel is a tiny nation, so small that her name has to be written in the sea on most maps. For decades, Israelis had been living with an enemy at every gate. For years, they had been walking in the shadow of bad news—the worldwide criticism, the troubled economy, the terrible misadventure in Lebanon.

Now, with the first news of Operation Moses, the siege lifted for a moment. From Dan to Eilat, from the northern tip to the southern edge of this little nation, there was euphoria. They had redeemed the falashas—and themselves.

Israel had remembered her reason for being. Time after time, "with a mighty hand," as the Passover verses say, "and an outstretched arm," she had reached for her scattered children. With Operation Magic Carpet, she had delivered the threatened Jews of Morocco and Yemen. With Operations Ezra and Nehemiah, she had airlifted other Jews from hostile Iraq. In the early 1970s, when Russia's gates were briefly ajar, she had gathered in some of the Soviet Jews. Now, with Operation Moses, the Ethiopians had been saved.

There was joy in the streets of Jerusalem. Yet, like so many Jewish celebrations, this one was bittersweet and haunted by the people who were missing.

There were still Jews struggling to stay alive in the refugee camps of Sudan. If one operation was over, a new one was desperately needed. Once again, Israel had to turn for help to her American friends.

In Washington, they pondered the problem. "How do we help those people now?" Some of the State Department men were still furious with the Israelis for having broken secrecy. They fretted about the damage done to U.S.-Arab relations. They argued about timing. "Let's wait," one top official urged, "until the situation cools down." Yet people were dying; if they waited too long, there might be no one left to rescue.

In the jargon of diplomats, they talked about "the sensitivities" of Sudan. Like witch doctors poring over entrails, they studied the messages from that country. "I won't help Israel by sending them more people," Nimeiry told a reporter. "But if they want to go away from here—to Europe, to the United States, to anyplace else—I don't care."

Was that a new crack in the door? There's a difference and a distance between words and deeds. In Israel, the words worried Yehuda Dominitz. "In our experience with the Arabs," he said, "when the words are soft, the action that follows is harsh. And vice versa."

As the Americans understood, the Sudanese were once burned and they were now twice shy. "If we do anything at all," a Sudanese official made it clear, "it can't be the same way as before."

Another elaborate operation, with all sorts of people involved, was impossible. If Sudan agreed to anything, it would have to be an all-American rescue. The CIA was mentioned. At one point a Sudanese leader had proposed that the CIA run the first airlift, but they demurred. They are an intelligence agency, not in the people-moving business. Now, they were the only organization that Sudan would trust to carry it off.

Meanwhile, on February 1, an impatient man arrived at the State Department. He was Phil Blazer, publisher of *Israel Today*. Over lunch with Richard Krieger of the Office of Refugee Affairs, Blazer unveiled a daring scheme of his own.

Within a week of the end of Operation Moses, Blazer had started to plan his own airlift. He called it Operation Joshua, after the Exodus leader who took over from Moses, the general who made the walls of Jericho "come tumbling down."

Blazer's idea was to lease a passenger jet and fly it to Khartoum, to bring out the stranded Ethiopian Jews. He'd already made a contact at Trans-American charter airlines. He'd recruited a group of doctors and nurses to fly with the plane and care for the sick passengers in midair. Even as he and Krieger were speaking, a member of Blazer's staff, Hal Sloane, was already in Sudan. Traveling undercover, disguised as a film executive, Sloane was poking around the refugee camps, trying to locate the Jews, get an accurate count of them, and map out a way to transport them to Khartoum.

Nervously, Krieger listened. "We are working on the situation," he interrupted. The plan sounded like a *Rambo* spinoff, and it was the State Department's nightmare. An American plane landing illegally in Khartoum. American citizens captured, perhaps killed. Krieger sympathized with the publisher's motives, but the scheme would never fly; such a plane would never be allowed to leave the United States.

Over coffee, Krieger pledged, "We are doing everything we can." When lunch was over, he had persuaded Blazer to "delay" his plan.

Yet Blazer was still impatient. "I'm going to talk to the vice-president," he said. Krieger nodded. He was planning the same thing himself.

Krieger talked with Vice-President George Bush. Until now, Bush had been briefed on the situation but not directly involved. Krieger was hoping to change that, and to take advantage of an African tour that Bush was planning, with Khartoum as his first stop.

Next, Krieger set up a meeting with himself, Howard Teicher of the National Security Council, and a vice-presidential aide. On his visit to Sudan, the vice-president would be discussing that country's many problems. Perhaps he could find a way to link a second rescue of the falashas with Sudan's need for American aid.

The three men agreed that this was feasible, but there was still spadework to be done at the State Department. If there were another rescue, some of the men at State wanted to follow the old route, a single TEA plane each day. Krieger and the others thought that wouldn't work a second time. They were pushing for "a one-shot," a mass airlift that would pick everybody up in a single trip.

The rescue was still in the talking stage. Never a man to wait idly, Blazer launched into a second plan. This was an intensive campaign of political pressure. It would leave the officials at the State Department cool and unmoved, but it would have a great impact on "the politicals" at the Capitol and the White House. "Let's be honest," a State Department official suggested. "If there hadn't been constant lobbying, would there have been a falasha rescue? If there was no pressure, no phone calls and letters, would anything have happened?"

Blazer is a man with contacts, and now he burned up the phone wires to friends and friends of friends. He was in daily phone contact with Nate Shapiro, the president of AAEJ. To lay the groundwork for his meeting with George Bush, Blazer telephoned entertainment mogul Jerry Weintraub, a close friend of the vice-president, and backed it up with a call to a Miami attorney, a friend of Bush's son. In mid-February, Blazer and Shapiro met with Senator Alan Cranston of California. Then Blazer talked by phone with Senator Al D'Amato of New York. The publisher was very persuasive.

A few days later, the two senators put the finishing touches on a secret letter addressed to President Reagan. In it, they praised the president for his "leadership role" in aiding African famine victims, including the airlift of Ethiopian Jews. They reminded him that some had been left behind:

Tragically, the survival of these people is in jeopardy and they are at special risk. Given the strong ties that exist between our government and the government of Sudan . . . we would urge you to seek President Nimeiry's permission for the immediate resumption of the airlift. We pledge our ongoing support and assistance in your efforts to speed up the rescue of the last remnant of a 2,500-year-old Jewish community, and look forward to your response.

Now something remarkable happened in partisan, disputatious Washington. Within forty-eight hours, the letter was signed by each of the one hundred members of the United States Senate. Cranston collected eighty signatures, going from office to office to gather most of them. D'Amato obtained twenty-six signatures. All tolled, because some eager senators signed twice, there were 106 signatures to the letter. Privately, with no leaks of the contents of the letter, Cranston delivered it to the White House on February 21.

The following day, Blazer met with George Bush. Blazer talked to him about the world's failure to do anything to save the Jews during the Holocaust. "Mr. Vice-President," he urged, "we can do now what we didn't do then." The vice-president promised to do whatever was possible. As he said, he was now "mobilized."

That was a Friday. A Bush aide was dispatched to CIA headquarters, to get them on board. On Monday, Bush talked to President Reagan about it. Later, one of Bush's aides would brief Phil Blazer on that conversation. As Blazer remembered the report, "Bush went to the old man. He said that [Secretary of State George] Shultz was hanging back on this but that he, Bush, wanted to move ahead. And Reagan decided, 'Go!' "

Four days after their meeting, both the president and the vice-president placed private calls to Senator Cranston, expressing their support for the airlift that the senate letter called for. In a speech to the National Press Club in Washington, Bush talked about his planned African trip. As he told the reporters, the Ethiopian Jews were on the list of issues he planned to discuss with Nimeiry.

On March 4, armed with authority and the outlines of a plan, Bush landed in Khartoum. The vice-president had a busy schedule, but he took a few minutes to pose for a photograph with Jerry Weaver, America's point man on Operation Moses. Bush signed it "with respect for a great humanitarian." That same month, Weaver was also given a "Superior Honor Award," signed by James Purcell of the State Department.

Bush is a shrewd negotiator and Nimeiry a sharp bargainer. More than ever, Sudan needed America's goodwill and economic aid. Nimeiry was planning one of his regular trips to Washington, hoping for a warm welcome at the White House and a friendly reception on Capitol Hill, from the very same senators who had signed that letter.

Over tea in the presidential office, their conversations were secret. By the time he left, though, Bush had Nimeiry's agreement to an airlift of the remaining Ethiopian Jews. In turn, Nimeiry had an agreement that it would be done by the agency that Bush had once headed, the CIA.

As Bush flew off to his next stop, word was passed from the White House to the U.S. Ambassador in Khartoum, Hume Horan. That night, March 8, the ambassador and Jerry Weaver met with the CIA station chief—known to the Sudanese as "Mr. Milton"—and his aide. Together, they worked out plans for a new rescue. Operation Sheba, named for the mother of

Ethiopia, was set in motion. Secrecy was more important than ever. So was speed. The White House had agreed with Krieger, and was asking for a quick, in-and-out operation.

The next day, Jerry Weaver took two U.S. Air Force pilots to check out a remote landing strip near Gedaref. The runway was short, only nine hundred meters long, a strip of red gravel with a tricky uphill grade.

Frowning, the pilots paced off the strip. Americans had landed here before, delivering food and medicine for the refugees in C-130 transports. If the winds were right, if the pilots were sharp, they could do it again.

In Khartoum, Nimeiry was saying as little as possible. Later, different people would remember being told different things. According to General Abdul-Rahman Swareddahab, then the defense minister, he was alerted that American planes would be landing in eastern Sudan, "to unload relief supplies." According to Omar el-Tayeb, the vice-president and security chief, Nimeiry told him it was "a political decision motivated by the desire of the United States." Nimeiry then ordered him to supervise the airlift.

President Reagan had asked for a hurry-up timetable of three or four days. Twelve days passed, though, before all the pieces of the plan were in place. Among the delays was the problem of finding the people they wanted to rescue.

In Tawawa, the quiet Ethiopian had returned. This time, there was no clamoring and no pushing. The Jewish refugees were surprisingly calm and patient. "They knew you would be back," explained Gideon.

After the first airlift, the Americans had thought that twelve hundred Ethiopian Jews were left in the Sudanese camps. As the weeks went by, they had narrowed the guess. Now they expected to be flying out about nine hundred people.

Where were they? Gideon was frantic. He knew that some had died and a few others had walked back to Ethiopia, to wait there for the next *aliyah*. When he checked the lists, he found that some names appeared more than once, confusing everything.

When they counted heads, they found fewer than five hundred in Tawawa. In a search of the other camps, they found five others and brought them to Tawawa. "There are more," Gideon insisted. "I know it." Yet when they couldn't be located, the rescue mission had to go ahead without them.

On the evening of March 21, Gideon and the quiet Ethiopian gathered up the remaining Jews of Tawawa. At the landing strip they were divided into six groups. Among the shrubs and thorn trees that bordered the runway, they huddled on the ground and waited through the night.

A harsh wind was blowing, the hot and dusty wind that the Sudanese call *harmattan*. Two American pilots stood by on the ground, with radio gear to link them to the planes that were already on the way. If the gusts continued this strong, the landing would be too tricky. On a mission like this, they couldn't risk a crashed plane. The Sudanese say the *harmattan* is "an evil wind." If it kept blowing, they would have to call off the operation.

Through the night, the strong wind blew. As dawn came up on March 22, the harsh gusts dwindled and then died. They could hear the planes circling overhead. Reportedly, home base for this fleet of nine C-130 transports was the U.S. Air Force base near Frankfurt, West Germany.

The first plane touched down on the gravel strip just before 6:00 A.M. Its engines were still running, churning up a cloud of red dust, as the first group of Ethiopian Jews was hurried on board. "Quick, quick," Gideon urged them. In less than twenty minutes, it was in the air again.

One at a time, the other planes landed, loaded their passengers, and took off. Gideon climbed aboard the sixth plane, with the last group of refugees. Because they had not found all the passengers they expected, three of the planes returned empty. By nine-thirty, the airstrip was once again remote and deserted.

The CIA men were uncorking champagne for a celebration in Gedaref. In Washington, other men congratulated themselves for an operation that went "better than we hoped."

The planes were still in the air when the phone rang in Van Nuys, California. "We've done it!" one of George Bush's aides told Phil Blazer. "The operation is a success!" Then, for a reason he didn't explain, he asked the publisher to keep the secret for three more days.

Five hours after takeoff, the planes were over the Israeli airport near the Red Sea port of Eilat. One by one, at half-hour intervals, they landed.

Tattered and dazed, some laughing, some weeping, some of them carried off on stretchers, many of them murmuring prayers, 482 passengers emerged. The prime minister of Israel, Shimon Peres, was there to welcome them. The American ambassador, Samuel Lewis, watched as his nation's planes brought these wanderers home.

Three days later, Phil Blazer learned why he had been asked to keep the secret awhile longer. All along, no matter what else was happening, the Mossad had kept people moving through its old pipelines. Operation Sheba wasn't over until March 25, when another 106 Ethiopian Jews filed onto a plane in Khartoum and were airlifted to freedom.

A few days later, Gideon walked through the bustling streets of Jerusalem with his wife, Esther. He gawked at the shops, the traffic, the crowd of white faces. Some of them stared back, smiling at the young black couple. *"Shalom,"* a soldier greeted Gideon. An Israeli Uzi was slung over his shoulder, instead of the Kalashnikov that had become so familiar to Gideon.

*"Mazel-tov,"* a woman wished Esther, now almost six months pregnant.

"In this place they are friendly to strangers," Gideon murmured.

Esther smiled. "In this place we are not strangers."

## Chapter 15

# A Plague of Locusts

IN THE MARCH of history, Operation Moses and Operation Sheba were only footnotes. Yet in Sudan and Ethiopia, in the United States and Israel, the results were long-lasting and the consequences unexpected.

In Sudan, a political *harmattan* blew. President Gaafar al-Nimeiry had collaborated in an act of decency and goodwill, the rescue of Ethiopian Jews. It happened just as other troubles were catching up to him. The country was close to economic collapse now, flooded with refugees, battered by internal dissension, and buffeted by the rebellion in the south.

Yet Nimeiry was cocky. After sixteen years as president, despite a number of assassination attempts, including some very near misses, he still rode through the streets of Khartoum in an open car and walked boldly into the crowds. He was an old hand at fending off coups. In one attempt, he was seized and scheduled to be shot. Left unguarded for a moment, Nimeiry managed to crawl out of a rear window. Coolly, he hailed a taxicab and drove through town to rally his supporters.

He had, as *The Economist* described it, "the footballer's art;

sprint in one direction until trouble looms, then whip off in the other." He had, for example, imposed his own version of Sharia, or Islamic law, in 1983. Under these stern fundamentalist rules, adulterers could be punished by stoning and drinkers of alcohol by whipping. Thieves could have a hand cut off. In January 1985, a man of seventy-six, an opposition leader who criticized Nimeiry, was hanged for "heresy." When that execution turned out to be unpopular, Nimeiry simply changed direction, arresting a group of Moslem Brothers and blaming the "excesses" on them.

Once a year, it was Nimeiry's habit to fly to the United States for medical treatment. Usually, he also paid a visit to Washington, D.C., to discuss the health of his nation. A couple of weeks after Operation Sheba, confident that he could ride out one more cyclone, Nimeiry went ahead with that year's planned American visit.

The day he left, there were bread riots in the streets of Khartoum. The protestors included students, laborers, professionals, every segment of Sudan society. Nimeiry counted on Omar el-Tayeb, vice-president and security chief, to handle it, but the storm had been brewing for a long time.

The day Nimeiry tried to return, April 6, 1985, his government was overthrown. On the way home, on a stopover in Cairo, he learned that a military committee had seized power from him. Nimeiry had to ask his Egyptian friends for political asylum.

Now Operation Moses was pulled front and center. The new regime used it to discredit the old government. Because it is against Sudanese law to have any dealings with Israel, they charged Nimeiry in absentia with "high treason." Then, in October 1985, the curtain went up on a show trial of Vice-President Tayeb. Four other high-ranking officials also were accused as "traitors," then pardoned in exchange for their testimony against Tayeb.

In the drama of the trial, the United States and Israel were the archvillains and money the motive. A parade of witnesses made some extraordinary charges. According to some of this testimony, the old regime had taken as much as $50 million in payments and bribes from Israel and America to allow Operations Moses and Sheba.

Meanwhile, Jerry Weaver had fractured security a bit, speaking prematurely about his role in Operation Moses to a *Los Angeles Times* reporter. The "evidence" at the trial included morsels lifted from those interviews with Weaver and his Sudanese aide. Weaver had to be hustled out of Sudan for his own safety, leaving Ambassador Hume Horan behind to face the storm in Khartoum.

The trial became Khartoum's major entertainment, televised day in and day out over the government-run station. In the streets, there were now anti-American demonstrations. The government ignored Horan's protest that the televising of the trial encouraged these demonstrations and were "a sign of ingratitude" for the large amounts of American money and food aid.

As a precaution, the embassy "drew down" or reduced its staff, sending some people home. As the trial continued, the new regime began a flirtation with Libya, and a growing number of terrorists, most of them Libyan or Libyan-sponsored, were spotted in the streets and coffeehouses of Khartoum.

The city was at fever pitch. A year after Operation Sheba, ten thousand people rallied in the streets of Khartoum to denounce the United States. An American, a communications officer at the embassy, was shot, suffering severe brain damage and partial paralysis. As fears grew over more Libyan-directed terrorist attacks, four hundred Americans gathered at secret locations and traveled under armed escort to the airport, to be flown home. A "travel advisory" was issued, declaring Khartoum "unsafe" for Americans.

Month after month, the trial continued. Dressed in white robes and turban, Tayeb listened to the proceedings, at times a smile playing on his lips. He laughed out loud at testimony that a CIA agent had deposited $2 million, reportedly donated by Jewish organizations, in his personal bank account in London, as an "installment for his services" in the airlift.

Tayeb denied taking bribes, but he did admit to having a London bank account where he deposited "contributions" from foreign friends. According to Tayeb, one of his fondest dreams was to build a new state security headquarters in Khartoum, and he had asked foreign governments to chip in and pay for the project. The American government has denied making such "contributions."

When his turn to testify finally came, Tayeb said that he simply followed Nimeiry's orders on the airlifts. He claimed to be unaware that the refugees were Ethiopian Jews, on their way to Israel.

"Poor Omar," his friends in Washington say today. He and Nimeiry conspired to commit a good deed. Now Sudan was turning into one of those places where, as the cynics tell us, "No good deed goes unpunished."

In April 1986, six months after the trial began, Tayeb was sentenced to two consecutive thirty-year prison terms. The prosecution, yearning for even sterner punishment, insisted that they would appeal.

In Washington, there was a warning: *"Be careful how you write about this."* A year after Operation Moses, even two years after, they were still trying to keep secrets, still worried about careers at stake and lives at risk.

The men at the State Department still needed anonymity, so that they could be dispatched to other posts and fulfill other missions. They guarded the names of those Sudanese who had helped in this operation and were still undercover. And in Washington and Jerusalem, they were fierce about keeping "trade secrets," the ways and means that had been used in Operation Moses and might be used again in other undercover rescues.

A few short months after Operations Moses and Sheba, Americans and Israelis were in Geneva again. Once more they were meeting secretly, this time hoping to save American lives.

In 1986 there were headlines around the world about a secret American operation that had begun a year earlier—a clandestine sale of arms to Iran. The deal was, in part, an exchange of military supplies for American hostages held by Iranian-linked terrorists in Lebanon.

Israel was America's secret partner in those undercover shipments, but the payoff was disappointing. Only three American hostages were released, and others were quickly kidnapped in their place. Nine years earlier, Israel had made a similar swap with Ethiopia, but a better bargain in human lives—120 Ethiopian Jews for two planeloads of military spare parts.

The Iran arms deal exploded in controversy. There were scandals about secret Swiss bank accounts, "cowboys" in the White House basement, and illegal funds diverted to Central America. In Iran, there were only elusive phantoms, instead of the new friends that the Americans had hoped to find among the "moderates." Unlike Operations Moses and Sheba, this opening to Iran had been carried out without the full knowledge of the State Department and without the support of Congress. Now the White House came under attack, and Israel was criticized for her role in this secret deal.

The operations were different, but there was an important link between Operation Moses and the Iran affair. "When we needed help with the Ethiopian Jews, the Americans said yes," Shimon Peres explained in Jerusalem. "So when they asked us to help with *their* hostages, we too said yes."

In Ethiopia, a plague of locusts descended in July 1986. It struck parts of the country like a biblical curse. In the days of

Moses, such a plague was not enough to persuade the pharaoh to let the people go out of Egypt. In the time of the Dergue, it was still not enough to open the doors of Ethiopia and let the last of the Beta Israel leave.

The plague did not last long, perhaps because the sad country had little food on which the locusts could feed. There was still civil war. There was widespread hunger, for Jew and gentile alike. For want of a few pennies' worth of antibiotics, children were still going blind from the simplest eye infections.

Today, by most estimates, ten thousand Jews are still trapped in Ethiopia. Ambober, the largest all-falasha village, once had fifteen hundred people; today there are fewer than five hundred. In a typical village such as Teta, where two hundred falashas once lived, there are now only twenty.

Yet there may be more, unknown and uncounted. Before the exodus began, a 1976 census counted twenty-eight thousand falashas, but it was only a random sampling and an educated guess. Some Ethiopia watchers think it was a low estimate, and they would not be astonished to find that as many as fifteen thousand are still left as "prisoners of the Torah." Whatever the number, they struggle to survive, scattered now in the three hundred villages that remain. More than ever, they are falashas, strangers and wanderers.

The most likely road, the one through Sudan, is closed, at least for now. On a map of Africa, it is hard to find another exit for the thousands who are left. Officially, the Israeli government is taking "the humanitarian approach," as Moshe Gilboa of the Foreign Ministry puts it, appealing to the Ethiopian government to help reunite the broken families. Unofficially, a veteran leader of the exodus says, "We will have to be creative." Yet as he sighs, "It is always easier to bring out the first few than the last few."

Since the end of Operations Moses and Sheba, a few have trickled out of Ethiopia, in legal and quasi-legal ways. Mossad agents are still in place. The AAEJ claims to have brought out about three hundred people in the last two years. Among them was *Kes* Hadani, a revered leader whose son has become the first Ethiopian rabbi in Israel.

Those who remain are a tragic population. The young and the strong, the breadwinners, are gone. Mostly, the ones who stayed behind are old people, women, and young children. More than ever, they are the poorest of the poor.

Many of the families are headed now by women. They are used to hard work, but they don't have the physical strength for Ethiopian agriculture, pushing a wooden plow across stony ground. If they can find a farmhand to hire, they have to pay him half the crop or more, leaving less than the mother needs to feed her children. Other families are led now by elderly men; with their grown-up brothers gone, the younger ones of thirteen or fourteen must leave school to help their aging fathers on the farm.

In this bleakness, an old man, leaning on a walking stick, trudged for most of a day to reach the post office in one of the larger villages of Gondar province. Here, with the coins that might have paid for a day's food, he bought an envelope and a stamp for the letter that a friend had helped him to write.

"Yes, I am alive," Rachamim Alemie told his wife, Malka, far away in Israel. "I am present but I am crying."

Nineteen members of the Alemie family had been detoured on the road to Sudan, arrested, and then scattered. Now they lived in despair. Rachamim could not return to his old village; his land and house had been given to someone else. Without his tools, he could not work as a blacksmith, nor could he find other work. He moved from village to village, but most of the familiar faces were gone. Finally, he found a cousin who made room in his *tukul* for Rachamim.

Like the rest of Ethiopia, the Beta Israel were at nature's mercy. In May 1986, the "small rains" of spring didn't come to Gondar province, and they missed the first harvest. In June, some rain did fall, followed by the locusts of July.

In August, the rains were heavy and the hilltops of Gondar were shrouded in mist. A group of tourists, organized by the North American Conference on Ethiopian Jewry, arrived in one small falasha village. Half-naked children, cold and shivering in the damp, ran to help the warmly dressed visitors down a muddy, slippery mountain path. A white-turbaned *kes* welcomed them with songs and prayers. In their handbags and knapsacks, the tourists carried clothing from America, at least one warm garment for every child of the village.

In that village, a seven-month-old infant was feverish with pneumonia. On their tour bus, the visitors took the child and her mother to the hospital in Gondar city, but it was too late. "If you'd brought her a few days earlier . . ." the doctor sighed. All they could do now was watch the young mother as she walked back to her village, empty-handed, weeping for the dead child.

That autumn, the air was heavy with the scent of ripe grain. Some parts of Gondar had their best crop in years. For those who managed to harvest it, there was a brief respite from hunger. Yet the food would not last them until the next harvest. Yet children would still be cold and hungry. Yet people would still grow sick from parasites, fungus infections, and diseases that are curable in other lands but can be fatal here.

Even as the people were threshing that year's grain, the government of Ethiopia issued a warning. They had "meteorological information" that indicated there would be another "serious famine" in 1987, especially in the exhausted northern areas where the last of the falashas live.

The central government of Ethiopia is antireligion, anti-Zionist, but not anti-Jewish. Not officially, at least. Old hatreds die slowly. In hard times, people look for scapegoats. In the aftermath of Operation Moses, because some of the falashas had tried to join the secret exodus, they were taunted as "lawbreakers" and "traitors." Their neighbors also had economic reasons to be angry at them. In Tigray province, for example, with almost all the Jewish blacksmiths gone, the price of farming tools had almost tripled. The synagogues were open but the falasha schools were closed. The teaching of Hebrew was still outlawed, because the government continued to see it as the language of departure, not as the language of prayer.

If they could manage to get to a government school, if there was one within walking distance, Jewish children were now permitted to attend. At school, they kept their Jewish identities as quiet as possible. Eager to learn, they worried about being teased and humiliated by the other children and even the teachers.

That fall, after the harvest, there was another respite, the observance of the Seged. This was the falashas' own holiday, unique to them. Seged, which means "to bow down," was a day that began in fasting, a mourning over the destruction of the Temple and a remembrance of another exile, when their forefathers were carried off to Babylon. It ended in an evening of feasting. Seged celebrated the prophecy that had kept them alive through the centuries. Those ancient Jews had returned from Babylon, and one day they, too, the last of the falashas, would return to Jerusalem.

That year, fifteen hundred people came to celebrate the Seged in the village of Ambober. They walked long distances, arriving from smaller, faraway villages, hoping for a reunion with family and friends they hadn't seen all year. They shed their fears about being identified as Jews and celebrated openly.

This year, there was no government intrusion, no presence of troops, and no speeches by government officials, as there had been at other recent festivals. Instead, Ethiopian schoolchildren were brought from a nearby village and lined up to observe this "cultural event."

Men, women, and children, the Jews marched to a mountaintop, a reenactment of Moses going up to Mount Sinai. All day long, under a blazing November sun, they fasted and prayed. The *kesoch* read from the Torah about the giving of God's law.

Then they turned to the Book of Nehemiah, which tells of the return from the Babylonian captivity:

*"Remember, I beseech thee, the word that thou commandedst thy servant Moses, saying, 'If ye transgress, I will scatter you abroad among the nations. But if ye turn unto me, and keep my commandments, and do them . . . yet will I gather thee from thence . . .'"* (Neh. 1:8–9)

As the sun was setting, they marched down from the mountain, singing and dancing. They returned their prayer books to the synagogue, a symbol of the Torah's return to the holy Temple and their own hoped-for return to Jerusalem. Still clinging together, remembering those who had gone ahead of them, they shared a feast.

They were joined by a small group of Americans. The food had been provided by the North American Conference on Ethiopian Jewry and other volunteer groups. The skullcaps that the men wore had been brought by them too. These white Jews had carried hope with them, a promise that these last few falashas would not be abandoned.

No one can say how these remaining people will be redeemed, or when. The Americans were there simply to say amen to an old falasha prayer:

*"Do not separate me, O Lord, from thy chosen, from thy joy, from the light and from the splendor. Let me see, O Lord, the light of Israel, and let me listen to the words of the just. . . ."*

# Chapter 16

# Promises Kept

REHOV ANELEVITCH. Malka Alemie can barely pronounce the Hebrew name for her street in the bustling city of Holon, minutes from Tel Aviv and, in the tiny country of Israel, just a quick hour from Jerusalem. Two years after Operation Moses, she is at home in this loud and lively neighborhood. Laundry hangs on window clotheslines, flapping in the Mediterranean breeze. Hebrew is spoken here in a babble of immigrant accents—Ethiopian and Russian, Yemenite and Yiddish, English and Hispanic.

Children race everywhere. Today they are chasing an old egg seller who hawks his wares from house to house. They circle him, hoping to make him splatter an egg or two. The stoop-shouldered man is used to them, and he plays their game, making a fierce face at the ringleader, six-year-old Tzion.

Tzion's giddy shouts echo through the courtyard, but his family isn't sure what to make of this hubbub. The boy is becoming "like an Israeli," and that pleases them. Yet in Ethiopia, no one would tease an old man. A loud voice, even from a child, would be a sign that all dignity and self-control are lost.

They hope the boy will remember the old Ethiopian ways, and sometimes he does. Eager, curious, spontaneous, he still knows when to be quiet and respectful. He storms up the stairs and bursts noisily into the Alemie apartment, looking for his mother, demanding a snack. Then, as he sees that the grownups are talking to a visitor, he comes to a quick halt and grows still as a statue. He doesn't move again until the visitor offers a piece of candy. With a nod from Malka, he approaches, wide-eyed and solemn, hands cupped in front of him. He cannot reach for the candy; the gift must be given, not taken.

In Ethiopia, even a chief *kes* would not have a *tukul* as big as Malka's three-room apartment in Holon. She lives here with her grandson Avi, a bright child but a daydreamer, distracted by worries over his parents, lost "somewhere in Ethiopia." Her teenage daughter, Mazel, a clever student in a youth village, pretty in a pink sweater and plaid skirt, is home for weekends.

Across the courtyard, in another square and squat apartment building, Eigal and Kohava live with their children. Young Tzion and Orit, now eight, bring home gold stars on their school papers. Eigal has started his first job, at a nearby factory. Kohava has a new *ankelba,* and an infant son dozes in it, a warm, reassuring weight on her back.

A few weeks earlier, family and friends had crowded into the apartment to celebrate the child's *bris,* the circumcision ceremony that reaffirms the covenant for each new generation. Instead of a straw birthing hut, the child was born in a modern hospital. Instead of staying apart for forty days, the mother was at the ceremony.

There were mounds of *injera* and dark bottles of Israeli beer. "Not as strong as our *tala,*" the men decided. The Ethiopian immigrants chanted "Addis Ababa," the song of new hope, and they showed their Israeli neighbors how to do the pecking, roosterish shoulder dance. When the circumcision was done, Malka threw her head back, exultant. This was no moment for staying quiet. She produced a shrill, piercing sound, *lu-lu-lu-lu,* ululating her joy in the old Ethiopian way. For the first time in more than two thousand years, a child of her line had been born in the Holy Land.

The Alemies have moved through a time warp. They have followed a prophecy across hundreds of miles of space, skipping hundreds of centuries of time, traveling from the *tukuls* of Ethiopia to arrive, as if overnight, in the world of modern technology.

One dizzying change followed another. Just a few hours after they landed in Israel, the Alemies no longer recognized themselves. A bus hurried them from the airport to an absorption center. Here, after their first meal in Israel, they shed the tattered garments of Ethiopia. They were brought to a room full of clothing and invited to take what they wanted. The Israelis are hard-pressed people, but hundreds of them had rushed to the absorption centers to donate new or almost-new garments for the immigrants. Malka changed into a brightly printed dress, choosing it not for the colors but for its modest length, down to her ankles. Suddenly, Eigal was in blue jeans and a T-shirt, and little Tzion was staring into a mirror, amazed by his own image in a high-fashion jogging suit and Adidas sneakers.

The next day, they changed their names. If the government was going to take care of them, it had to keep track of them, but the Beta Israel had arrived without family names. In Ethiopia, each person had two first names, his own and his father's. Yonah Bogale's son, for example, was called Zachariah Yonah. At marriage, women did not change their names. In a single family, husband and wife, parents and children, all had different last names.

Now they were assigned family names, usually the name of the last male relative who had died. Alemie had been the name of Rachamim's father, and now they would all use it. At the urging of social workers, many of them also Hebraicized their first names as well.

*"Ishi, ishi,"* they said. "Yes, yes." They were eager to please. They were in a hurry to become Israeli. Yet they were also proud and stubborn. Among themselves, most of them continued to use their old Ethiopian names.

For Malka, those first months in Israel passed in a blur of marvels and mysteries. Suddenly, the grandmother was a student, rushing from class to class, learning a new language, the customs of a new country, the ways of a new century.

"In our village," she said, "we had heard about electricity." Now a social worker showed her how to turn night into day by pressing a switch. To get water, she turned a faucet, so much easier than carrying the heavy jugs from a spring. She rode on her first elevator, cooked her first meal on a gas stove, spoke on her first telephone.

If she didn't understand how these modern devices worked, neither do most people, even those of us who grew up with them. Learning to use these gadgets was the easy part. Learning to live in a new time and a new place was harder, slower, and more painful.

Even the voice of Israel was a culture shock. It was loud to Ethiopian ears, and Malka often thought the social worker or the teacher was yelling at her in anger. What have I done wrong? she wondered. The white Jews were friendly, helpful, but puzzling. They were harried, with no time for amenities, but Malka and her people needed at least five minutes to say hello with proper courtesy.

"In our villages, we did not know what Israel would look like. They told us it was a land of milk and honey." Smiling, Malka added, "And it is." There was abundance here. Most people ate meat every day, and there were fruits and vegetables Malka had never seen before.

Yet her world was turned inside out. Like most immigrants, no matter where they come from, Malka missed the comforting taste of familiar foods. She scoured the markets for a pepper as

hot as the fierce *burberri* peppers of Ethiopia. She tried one
Israeli grain after another, but nothing was like the *teff* of
Ethiopia, and nothing could produce *injera* that tasted quite
right.

"We were told we were coming to a Jewish land," she said
disapprovingly. She was astounded to see cars driving along on
the Sabbath, and people dressed as if they were going to the
beach. In her village, there was no such thing as a nonobserving
Jew; anyone who did not follow the laws was banished.

Like Malka, many of the Ethiopians had resented the long
years that it took Israel to recognize them as Jews. Now some
of them decided that they were "more Jewish," more faithful
and observant, than the Israelis. In one youth village, an Ethiopian student complained about a fire engine roaring by on a
Saturday. "But they have to put out the fire," she was told.
"No, no," she insisted. "If a house is burning on the Sabbath,
it is God's will."

Simple things had become complicated. Many of the younger
women did not know what to do when they had a menstrual
period in Israel, or where to go. There was no separate menstrual hut. "That's a custom from the days of the Temple," they
were told. "We don't do it anymore." They tried to understand,
but many husbands and wives found it strange to stay together
during those "unclean" times. Some of the women disappeared
for a few days each month and were found crouched in stair-
wells or hiding in clothes closets.

No one had ever seen Jews like these. Many of the women
arrived with tattoos, usually a necklace or two of blue designs.
Some had tattoos on their foreheads, a circle, a star, sometimes
a cross. That startled the Israelis, and the Ethiopians tried to
smooth it over. "The missionaries made us do it," some of them
explained. Or they said they did it themselves, "to look like a
Christian," because Jewish girls were a rape target. Sometimes,
with a shy smile, they told the truth. Religious symbols, the

cross or the Star of David, were blurred in Ethiopia. As young girls, wanting to be "in style," they'd copied this design from their Christian neighbors.

The Ethiopians did not like to complain, and the Israelis often had to guess at what the problem was. At first, husbands and wives were placed in the same *ulpan,* or Hebrew class, but the men lagged behind, learning hardly anything. Eventually, the teachers understood that Ethiopian men consider it undignified to study and perhaps compete with their own wives. Placed in a different class, still coed but without his wife, the man caught up quickly.

There were now about sixteen thousand Ethiopian Jews in Israel. For the white Jews, there was something mystical about the arrival of this lost tribe, forgotten for so many centuries, clinging to their faith, redeemed at last. Their story was stranger than fiction, better than fiction.

They were met with an outpouring of love. Volunteers flocked to the absorption centers, wanting to do something for these new immigrants. Many of them "adopted" an Ethiopian family, taking them shopping, escorting them to synagogue, bringing them home to dinner.

For the government of Israel, human concerns were complicated by politics. The arrival of the black Jews, and the warmth and caring with which they were received, put an end to the old charge that "Zionism is racism." Yet Israel still winced under that accusation.

With Operation Moses, so many people arrived so quickly, so secretly, that the system wasn't ready for them. Many of them, including the Alemies, had to be placed in an Israeli version of "welfare hotels," sagging buildings that had been converted into makeshift immigrant centers. The hotels broke up the pattern of family life. As the Israelis knew, these people would have been happier in family-size tents than in those bleak, cramped rooms. Yet as the government officials explained, "We can't have the world pointing and saying, 'Look how Israel treats the black people. Look how they put Africans in tents.' "

The Alemies spent their first months in an aging hotel in Natanya. As quickly as possible, they were moved out of those dreary rooms and given apartments of their own. Each apartment cost the government about forty thousand dollars and was furnished with the necessities: stove and refrigerator, beds, a table and chairs. Some veteran Israelis grumbled about that, as they do about the cost of every immigration.

"They give them too much," some people complained. "It's true," admitted Jacob Tsur, Minister of Absorption. "We are giving them more than we gave other immigrants, because they come here with more problems. We want to get them off to a decent start."

Again, there were political considerations. Every other ethnic community has at least one place in Israel—a town, a neighborhood, a collective farm—where large numbers of their people live together and preserve their traditions and identity. Some of the Ethiopians would have wanted to cluster together, re-creating the old village life in this new land, but it wasn't possible. Deliberately, they were scattered, ten families here and ten there. As Jacob Tsur explained, "We cannot create a black ghetto."

For Malka, politics would come later. First, there were cultural leaps to make. She watched Eigal with a special concern. As she realized, it was harder for the men to get started in this new life than for the women. Once they had apartments and kitchens of their own, Malka and Kohava had their old jobs back. They were doing it differently, but they were still cooking, cleaning, and caring for their children. Eigal, though, felt displaced and restless. He would never do his traditional work again. Israel had no need of blacksmiths, and farming was different here, scientific and mechanized. His past was gone and suddenly he had to choose a future. Without an education, the options were limited. He went through a job-training course, learning low-level skills, feeling impatient. He wanted to be working, earning money, acting as provider and head of his family once again.

He had "work habits" to learn. He'd come from a timeless society to a land of clocks. If there was a job to be done in Ethiopia, it didn't matter if you did it tomorrow or the day after. They worked at nature's pace. They drove themselves hard at planting and harvesting. At other times, there was no reason to rush, and little reward for working harder. If you grew more crops, the landlord took most of the harvest; if you forged more tools, the prices were low and the customers few.

In Israel, everyone was in a hurry. If they expected you at nine o'clock, they were angry if you came at noon. If a man was away from his job for two or three days, to celebrate a friend's wedding, they didn't understand. Here they expected you to live by a schedule. Here there were reasons—more money, perhaps a better job—to work harder.

The Israelis too were learning. "We made mistakes in the past with other immigrants, and we don't want to repeat them," said Haim Aron of the Jewish Agency. "When the Moroccans came, we told them, 'Forget who you were in the old country. You are starting a new life here.' Now we are telling the Ethiopians, 'Bring your culture with you. Be who you are.'"

In Israel, Malka Alemie was not always sure who she was. She had left village life behind. She was being told to change her religious practices. Everything in Israel—the language, the clothes, the food, the houses—was new to the Ethiopians. An ancient people in a modern land, what was left of who they used to be?

On the Sabbath, Malka dressed in her Ethiopian *kamise,* wrapped her head in her best white scarf, and led her family to the synagogue. Unlike every other wave of immigrants, the Ethiopians did not organize a synagogue of their own, a place where they could follow their own rituals and traditions. Instead, obediently, they were trying to "normalize" their religion and follow the rituals of other Jews.

The congregation welcomed them. Eigal, still struggling to learn Hebrew, could not read from the Torah, but he was given other synagogue honors. Malka smiled proudly as her son carried the Torah or opened the curtains of the Ark. She was amazed by a service in which people sat, then stood, then sat again; in Ethiopia, only the *kes* had a chair. She held a prayer book on her lap, turning pages she couldn't read, listening to a language that was still foreign to her. "I don't always know when to say amen," she said with worry.

"We must hurry to catch up," she told her family. Yet this was the hardest change of all, the eternal dilemma of the immigrant. In the rush to become Israelis, what would happen to their own traditions? "The children know more than the parents," she said, half proud, half uneasy.

Quick to learn, the children became the voice of the family, translating between them and the immigration officials. Often they saw their parents in the role of children, bewildered and uncertain, listening to other groups, white Jews who told them what to do.

Malka worried about that. She embraced this new land, but she clung to old values. "If the children lose respect for their parents," she said, "we lose everything." For Tzion and the other Alemie children, my interviews with their parents were rare events. A white stranger was listening carefully, respectfully, to them. For a change, they were the experts, with knowledge to share, with important things to say.

"Who are we now?" Malka kept asking. "Our old ways were good for us," she insisted. "They kept us together. They helped us to survive. Must we forget them now?"

Looking for an answer, Malka traveled to the great synagogue of Jerusalem. She stared at the massive stone building that was also the headquarters of the chief rabbinate. In a small park across the road, hundreds of Ethiopians were camped out.

Her people were "on strike," something Malka had never heard of before. They were walking out of their *ulpans,* pouring out of their absorption centers, arriving by the busload. Men, women, and children, they were a stubborn presence, demonstrating against the rabbis who said they were Jews, but with a string attached. The rabbis wanted them to go through a special ceremony of immersion, in the sea or at a *mikvah* or ritual bathhouse—to wash away the "irregularities" of Ethiopia.

Ironically, the rabbis had once been the best friends the Ethiopians had. By recognizing them as Jews, the descendants of the lost tribe of Dan, the rabbis had made it possible for them to come to Israel. Yet when the first few arrived, the rabbis had demanded that they submit to an elaborate ceremony.

At first, that ceremony had included a symbolic circumcision, a new cutting for the men who had been circumcised in Ethiopia when they were eight days old. As hundreds and then thousands of them arrived, the Ethiopians began to feel strong enough to say no to this ritual. As word of the symbolic circumcision spread, other Israelis were also indignant. "We have the nerve to call *them* primitive," novelist Amos Elon protested, "when the first thing we do when they arrive is to take a drop of blood from their penises!"

Just as Operation Moses was getting under way, that demand was dropped. Now, only a ritual immersion was being asked. Yet the strike was being led by young men who had been among those first arrivals. Some of them had been through the symbolic circumcision, and they still burned with humiliation over it. They urged the others to boycott the *mikvah.* "We were Jews in the past," they argued, "and we are Jews now."

The rabbis agreed. The question was not whether the Ethiopians were Jews but whether some of them had married non-Jews and others of them were "illegitimate"—because of the "irregularities" in their marriage and divorce customs. By Jewish law, a *momser,* or bastard, is not a child born out of wedlock; it is a child born to a married woman who has a love affair or who takes a second husband before she has been properly divorced from the first one. Because Ethiopian marriages and divorces did not always follow the rabbinical law of Israel, the rabbis were insisting on an immersion ceremony, to wash away any "taint" of the past.

The rabbis called it "a renewal of the covenant," but to the Ethiopians it sounded like a conversion ceremony. They heard echoes of past terrors in it. In Ethiopia they had struggled against the missionaries who wanted to baptize them. Now they found themselves battling the rabbis of Israel.

"It is a shameful thing," Malka protested, "to say we are less than other Jews." As she asked, "When the messiah comes, will they send him to the *mikvah* too?"

Yet that day at the strike, Malka smiled at the scene. A public protest was new to her people, but they brought their own traditions to it. By day, under the blazing sun of a Jerusalem September, with thousands of them crowded together, they were calm and quiet. In the chill of the Jerusalem night, with hundreds of them still there, sleeping on strips of cardboard, they kept their discipline and their dignity.

For most of the white Jews who passed by, it was their first encounter with black Jews. With the strike, the Ethiopians emerged from the isolation of the absorption centers. Now they were telling Israel who they were, and the rest of Israel answered.

Farmers from a kibbutz drove up with truckloads of fruits and vegetables for the strikers. A local butcher arrived with a supply of salamis. "It's Friday," he said. "They need food for the Sabbath." Some people brought gifts of warm clothing, and the municipality of Jerusalem lent blankets. "We'll be lucky if we get seventy-five percent of them back," the officials told each other. Yet when the strike was finally over, the Beta Israel returned more neatly folded blankets than they'd been given.

Some people came to argue with the strikers. In soft mur-

murs, the Ethiopians answered questions, but now and then their anger flared. In one discussion, a young man pulled the skullcap from his head and threw it on the ground. He would no longer wear the emblem of people who insulted him.

Others came to agree with them. "Listen," a white woman, a Holocaust survivor, told Malka. "If your son has to be immersed, my son will go with him. All of us will walk into the sea with you."

"Even the rabbis?" Malka asked.

For a month, even through the holiest days of the year, Rosh Hashana (the New Year) and Yom Kippur (the Day of Atonement), they sat there in protest. At one time or another, almost every member of the Beta Israel took part in the demonstration. They ran the strike as if it were a village dispute, to be talked about and decided together. Each day the leaders would report on their negotiations to the hundreds of people in the park. Anyone who wanted to could have his say. Then the entire assembly voted on what to do next.

As the strike dragged on, some Israelis grew impatient. The Ethiopians were stubborn, but that was how they had survived for so many centuries. The rabbis too were stubborn, insisting that the Halacha, or oral laws, were "not negotiable." Both sides were sincere but unyielding.

The Ethiopians blinked first. Finally, they voted to end their strike. There was a vague agreement that the immersion ceremony would not be required for all Ethiopians, only for those who wanted to get married. The status of these brides and grooms would be decided on a case-by-case basis. Yet it took more than a year for a rabbinical court to be set up for that purpose.

The Ethiopian priests had detailed histories of most families. Because they had been so strict about marriages between relatives, even third or fourth cousins, they had kept careful genealogies, going back as far as six or seven generations. With the testimony of a village *kes,* an Ethiopian could prove his lineage better than most other people could. Yet the *kesoch* were excluded from the court.

Seventeen *kesoch* had arrived in Israel, but, like the blacksmiths and the weavers, their jobs were obsolete here. Some were studying to be rabbis, and others were training to be ritual supervisors. As *kesoch,* they had moral authority but no legal standing to perform marriages or other religious ceremonies in Israel.

The strike had settled very little—except in Malka's mind. She had found her answer. "In some ways, we do not have to change," she told her family. Her people could do something new, like this strike, and still be themselves, still proud and disciplined, still calm and dignified.

Whatever the rabbis said, she had seen something important in that Jerusalem plaza. "The people of Israel are with us," she understood now. "I can see on their faces that we are different, but I also see that we are sisters and brothers."

Here and there, there have been problems about color. On a bus, a few people still stare. Some are quick to say that they do not want their sons or daughters to marry any of these newcomers. In an apartment building in Ashdod, the white residents locked the doors against the black Jews who were moving in.

That was a rare event, unusual enough to make headlines. The Jews of Israel have been gathered in from every corner of the world. The pioneers were the white Jews of Europe. When the second wave came, the dark-haired, olive-skinned Jews of Morocco and Yemen, *they* were called "black Jews." With time, that discrimination has faded, and the Israelis have grown used to diversity. Today, the tones of their skin, the colors of their hair, the shapes of their noses, all are different. On a crowded street, it is hard to say who "looks Jewish."

When the Alemies arrived on Rehov Anelevitch, they were met by welcome signs, crayoned by the children, and hot food, prepared by their mothers. Two years later, there's still a busy traffic of old and new neighbors. A child comes looking for his playmate, Tzion. A woman knocks at Malka's door.

"Are you at home?" she calls out.

"*Ishi, ishi,*" Malka answers. "Yes, yes."

"Where do you live in Jerusalem?" White-haired Yonah Bogale smiles at the question from an Ethiopian woman. For his people, the name of the city is still their name for all of the promised land.

For Yonah, the answer is a tree-lined street in Petah Tikvah, a town in the lowland center of Israel. He might have preferred an apartment in Jerusalem itself, but its cold winters make his old bones ache. Here, the mild climate reminds him of Ethiopia.

He is eighty years old now, frail, slow-moving, but still erect. He is a semiretired patriarch, still honored as the teacher and leader who prepared his people for the *aliyah.*

A large table dominates his living room. He is busier than many people half his age, doing translations and writing articles. On Friday, he clears away the books and papers and sets candlesticks on the table. His family is coming, all six of his sons, with their families, to spend the Sabbath with him. He also has two daughters, one of them studying to be a nurse in Canada, the other still a hostage with her mother in Ethiopia.

Foreign visitors still call on him. Israeli officials still fetch him, wanting his familiar face on the dais at important occasions. For fifty years he was the Beta Israel's spokesman, their link with the other Jews of the world, and he is still their best-known citizen in Israel. Yet as he says, "I am not so involved. It is up to a new generation now." Two of his sons have emerged as leaders of that generation.

Yonah has passed the torch, but he keeps a wary eye on his people. He paid careful attention as the Israeli government drew up a "master plan" for them, with a different forecast for each age group.

Half of the Ethiopians who came to Israel, about seven thousand of them, are children under the age of eighteen. They are the great hope, bright and shining, of the Beta Israel. As soon as they mastered the language, they were moved into the mainstream of Israeli education. "After half a year," according to Jacob Tsur, Minister of Absorption, "most of them reach the average level of the school system."

Some of them learn even faster. In one youth village, the Ethiopian children covered five years of learning in one, to catch up with their age group. In a different school, the children were upset when they were given crayons to draw pictures. "We came to learn," they insisted, "not to play." Their good manners have dazzled the Israelis. Some of them come early to class, in case the teacher has a few extra minutes to give them, and they stay late, to thank the teacher.

"Our children work very hard," Yonah half agrees, half boasts. Their oral traditions have given them sharp memory skills, and they are hungry for learning. Yet there also are problems. Many of them are still haunted by the terrors of the refugee camps in Sudan. Others suffer from a survivor's guilt, and they are distracted by memories of parents, brothers, or sisters who didn't make it. As youngsters, they are learning the new language quickly, but it is still a new language. Yet as youngsters, there are no limits to their possibilities.

For the second group of Ethiopians, those between eighteen and twenty-eight or so, education is also the answer. There are special programs for the twenty-five hundred in this age group, with government help for everyone who wants to study. Some are going to school for the first time in their lives. Some are studying things they never heard of in Ethiopia. At Hadassah Hospital in Jerusalem, a group of young immigrants are training to become dental assistants. When the class began, they were asked how many of them had ever been to a dentist before, and only one young woman raised her hand.

Others are picking up their education where they left off in

Ethiopia, finishing high school, going to preparatory schools, moving on to special technical schools or a university. "Each according to his own will," says Tsur, "and his own ability."

For those over thirty or thirty-five, the problems are thornier. For most of them, Hebrew is their first written language, and the job skills they can learn are low-level and middle-level. In some factories, they are getting on-the-job training. In other industries, the government subsidizes special programs that help the new immigrants to climb a few rungs on the job ladder.

Eigal Alemie is at the young end of this group. He struggles to support a growing family on a factory wage. Yet this is just his first job, and he hopes for a promotion. "It is very important that some of these people advance," Tsur explains. "By fixing your place in the new job or profession, you fix your place in Israeli society."

Malka is at the far end of the group, the people in their fifties and sixties who are called "the generation of the desert." In every wave of immigrants, there always are older people who can't make it on their own in the new land, who will always need and receive assistance from the government and from their families.

How will it be for my people? Yonah wonders. It is time for a new prophecy. As he knows, the Beta Israel will rise or fall with their homeland. If Israel thrives, so will they. If there are enough jobs for everyone, they will prosper. If there is peace, one day they will live in it.

Yet Israel struggles today. Under the master plan, the government has tried to avoid settling the new immigrants in the towns and cities that have social problems and high unemployment. Instead, they've been scattered in fifty cities, towns, or neighborhoods, no fewer than 100 to 150 families in a neighborhood, so they won't be lonely, but no more than 250 to 300 in any one place, so they won't create a ghetto.

Yonah nods. It is a good plan, but easier to write down than to carry out. "Yes, we have many problems, but my people are happy to be in the promised land," he says. "It is a miracle that we have been brought home. It is the beginning of the redemption. It means the messiah will surely come."

Once his people thought the messiah would be black; now they suspect he will be white. "No matter." Yonah smiles. "As long as he comes."

"We are falashas no more." Gideon smiles his crooked smile. Now he is street-wise in Israel, loping along the broad avenues of Ramat Aviv, the neighborhood that surrounds Tel Aviv University. For Gideon, the promised land has kept its promises. "Or most of them," he says.

For their first months in Israel, Gideon and Esther were dizzy with joy. Their child was born, a beautiful daughter. "Think of it," Gideon murmured. "She will never be a stranger."

Her parents were rushing to become Israelis themselves. At his *ulpan,* the bridegroom of Ethiopia wrote an essay about marriage among the Beta Israel, and won first prize in a nationwide contest for new immigrants. Before long, they were enrolled in preparatory classes for the university, Gideon planning to study computer sciences and Esther to major in economics.

Yet, like most of their people, they were riding an emotional roller coaster. Most immigrants, no matter where they come from, no matter what country they arrive in, live through this emotional curve. For the first few months, there is euphoria. Then there's a period of letdown, of sadness and confusion. There are changes to work through and adjustments to make before life can return to an even keel.

For Gideon, reality was setting in. In Ethiopia, he'd been a member of the elite, racing ahead of his people in education. In Israel, his school transcript didn't measure up. In Sudan, he'd lived a masquerade, winking, lying, slipping through the night to survive. Now, there was no bluffing his way through the quizzes and exams of an Israeli school.

He struggled to keep pace with his classmates but, like a number of other Ethiopians, he had to repeat some of his classes. "We must work very hard," he told Esther. Yet while she stayed home, studying after she'd put the baby to bed, he often had other things to do.

Gideon was still a night shadow, shuttling now between Tel Aviv and Jerusalem, still carrying messages for his people. They were no longer secret words, but public and political. In Ethiopia, the elders had been the leaders. In Israel, it was young men like Gideon who were competing to become the new leaders of their people. Almost overnight, the Ethiopians waxed political, and Gideon became an officer in one of the dozen or so Beta Israel organizations.

"So many organizations." An Israel official laughed. "It's how we knew they were really Jewish." Gideon and Esther didn't laugh when they heard that story. They were touchy. "We have always been Jewish," they insisted. "We don't need to prove it."

Real life, though, is full of ironies. Faith and religious passion led them to the Holy Land. Now that they've arrived, they may lose some of that zeal. In Ethiopia, they kept their identity by being separate and different from other people. Now that pressure is gone; they are in "the land of the Jews," and it is a secular place, for the most part. The earliest immigrants are less and less observant and strict about the laws. Even among some of the newcomers, especially the young people, there are signs of a falling away.

As a blessing and a curse, these are stubborn people. They may grow less strict and severe about it but, as they say, "We were Jews in the past, and we will be Jews in the future." Their argument with the rabbis continues, a wound that won't heal. Even for people who are already married, like Gideon and Esther, it is a personal insult.

For now, they are quiet about it, and the issue has gone underground. On their trek out of Ethiopia, they dodged bandits and government troops. Now they are looking for ways to outflank the rabbis. Some young people are living together without marriage. A few have gone quietly to the *mikvah*, in order to marry. A few others have found a *kes* or a friendly rabbi to marry them, without the *mikvah* ceremony, and no one talks about how such marriages become registered.

Yet in Israel, where most Ethiopians still need government help, especially in finding a place to live, it's important to be legal and official. There are no civil marriages here, and the chief rabbis have full control over such issues as marriage and divorce. They are as unbending as the Ethiopians. For now, it is a problem without a solution, but they are used to that in this part of the world.

Gideon and Esther kept the Sabbath, but separately. She stayed close to home with the baby, while he spent the day praying and talking with friends. In Ethiopian style, they were still living sex-segregated lives. After all the disguises he'd worn, Gideon was finding it hard to shuck the old habits of patriarchy.

Gideon was named for the falasha kings, but Esther was named for Judaism's most famous queen. "In Ethiopia, the man is king," a friend tried to explain to them, "but in Israel, the woman is queen." They'd been married as strangers, and now they were clashing royally over the new roles of men and women.

They were barely getting by on small scholarships from the Jewish Agency, living in a rented room with kitchenette, about the size of a *tukul.* When Gideon's friends came to visit, Esther was demure, eyes cast down, smiling shyly. She served coffee, then retired to her corner. Yet this docility came harder and harder. She'd been an "old virgin," with high hopes even in Ethiopia. Now, in her sweater and plaid skirt, knee socks and running shoes, she wanted something different and more equal.

She was proud of Gideon. He had guided them to freedom, and he was still a leader of their people. She smiled when he rode their little daughter around on his shoulders, but it wasn't enough. She was trying to be wife, mother, and student, and she wanted help with the housework, the shopping, the child care. "Israeli men do that," she argued. "It's not proper," he insisted, close to shouting. He was on his way to a political meeting, and the door slammed behind him.

The tension grew. Gideon was edgy, nostalgic for the high drama of his spying days, disappointed with his progress at school, harried by the demands of his political work. The arguments became more frequent. By the time their little daughter was taking her first steps, they were walking away from each other. It was a trial separation, and perhaps they would find their way back.

For now, Gideon packed his few clothes and his collection of hats—the fedora from Juba, a baseball cap, a wool helmet. He took with him his proudest treasure, a plaque presented by the AAEJ to a young man "who gave of himself so that Ethiopian Jews might live in freedom and dignity." On the top of the plaque, a quotation from Maimonides is inscribed: "He who saves a human life, it is as if he had saved a whole world."

The Ethiopian Jews arrived in Israel without baggage, but they did not come empty-handed. Ragged and starving, they carried with them a gift of faith, and the proof that it can endure. For all the world to see, here was living evidence that the human spirit can prevail, even in darkness.

They brought other gifts—their traditions, their courtesies, their music, dances, and crafts. In Israel, there are centers where they can practice their skills in weaving and pottery. There is a fledgling dance troupe, and the old musicians are teaching younger ones. In some schools, the children are taught Amharic along with Hebrew, and a small Ethiopian yeshiva has been opened, to train rabbis and teachers in both the old and new cultures.

The Queen of Sheba came to Jerusalem bearing gifts of gold and rare spices. The Ethiopian Jews brought something more precious, the gift of the Seged, their celebration of faith and God's promise. Every wave of immigrants has brought a special holiday with them. As the Israelis say, "Each one adds a pearl to the crown."

For generations, they kept this day in exile. Now, in the autumn, they gather in Jerusalem, men, women, and children marching together. The *kesoch* carry the old ceremonial umbrellas, embroidered fantasies of red and green silks. Men beat the ancient drums and gongs they have carried from Ethiopia.

Some white Jews walk with them, sharing a day that begins in sadness, fasting, and prayer. In this remnant of a lost tribe, almost every person has a parent, a child, a brother or sister left behind in Ethiopia.

Where is my husband? Malka thinks. Where are my daughters? As she marches, are they marching too? As she climbs a Jerusalem peak, are they on a mountaintop in Ambober? At this same moment, does Rachamim stand, wrapped in his *shamma,* bowing his head with all those others who are still falashas, still trapped in Ethiopia?

The Seged ends in an evening of feasting and celebration. In Jerusalem, the final prayers are said at the Wailing Wall, the western wall that is all that remains of the old Temple.

Finally, Malka Alemie stands where her ancestors once prayed. For more than two thousand years her people yearned to return to this spot. Her hand trembles as she touches the ancient stones. Around her, other women murmur prayers in Hebrew, but Malka worships in the language of Ethiopia. God will understand, she knows. As is the custom, she wedges a piece of paper, a prayer, between the old stones.

No one knows better than she that prayers are answered. She stands in Jerusalem, redeemed, a stranger no more.

A few feet away, Gideon slips his own prayer between the sunstruck stones. For him, there are still plans to make, still exits to find for the last of his people. One day, other hands will touch these stones. One day, the secret exodus will be over.

# *INDEX*

# About the Author

CLAIRE SAFRAN is a roving editor for *Reader's Digest*. She has published articles on a wide range of topics in such major magazines as *Woman's Day, Parade, Redbook,* and *TV Guide*. She is a former executive editor of *Redbook,* editor-in-chief of *Coronet,* associate editor of *Family Weekly,* and copy girl for the *Jewish Daily Forward*.

She has won numerous awards for her writing, including the American Society of Journalists and Authors Award for Outstanding Magazine Article and the William Harvey Award, and she is a three-time winner of the Odyssey Institute Media Award. She has also won writing awards from the American Psychological Foundation, the Religious Public Relations Council, the American Academy of Pediatrics, the American Academy of Family Physicians, and Women in Communications.

Safran is a graduate of Brooklyn College. She currently resides in Connecticut with her husband, photographer and communications historian John Milton Williams. Their son, Scott Williams, is a composer and lead guitarist with the rock group Macchu Picchu.